Praise for *Supercoach*

"Michael Neill, a supercoach in real life, has used h~
writing talent to cause this book to re~
shoulders and shake you till y

— **Steve Chandler,**
Motivate Yourself

"Reading **Supercoach** is lik _____ ~~..~~ ~est friend
on hand, passing on solid adv~~...~~c each time you read. How
many 'nuggets' does it take to make a gold mine? The
answer in terms of wisdom is contained herein."

— **Andy Fowler,** Emmy Award–winning visual-effects producer of
The Life and Death of Peter Sellers

"Michael Neill has a rare gift for blending theory and practice
into an enjoyable and helpful read. Whether you're interested
in coaching, being coached, or just thinking and smiling
about your path through life, I recommend this book."
— **David Glazer,** director of engineering, Google

"This book is one of the best, if not <u>the</u> best, book on coaching
that I have ever read. What is so interesting about **Supercoach**
is that you do not need to be a coach to benefit from reading it—
you simply need to be alive. It is more than 250 pages of pure written
gold. The stories, exercises, and 'in a nutshell' summaries are simply
powerful; and this book will be a gift to so many."

— **Steve Hardison,** personal, business, and relationship coach,
www.theultimatecoach.net

"Michael has completely outdone even himself with this book.
This is simply one of the best self-help books I've ever read, and certain
to be a classic for years to come. Michael's words go straight to the
heart. By reading this book, you will feel lighter, more joyful, and more
able to enjoy this life in this moment."

— **Jennifer Louden,** the author of *The Life Organizer*
and *The Woman's Comfort Book*

"**Supercoach** is a perfect guide to help you navigate from
thought to possibility to intention to results. This is much
more than a 'feel-good' read—this book is transformational.
Read it and go make a difference!"

— **Rob Owen,** adjunct professor, Thunderbird
School of Global Management.

Supercoach

Also by Michael Neill

Books

FEEL HAPPY NOW!

THE INSIDE-OUT REVOLUTION: Two Things You Need to Know to Change Your Life Forever (available April 2013)

YOU CAN HAVE WHAT YOU WANT: Proven Strategies for Inner and Outer Success

CD Program

EFFORTLESS SUCCESS: How to Get What You Want & Have a Great Time Doing It (6-CD set)

All of the above are available at your local bookstore,
or may be ordered by visiting:

Hay House UK: **www.hayhouse.co.uk**
Hay House USA: **www.hayhouse.com**®
Hay House Australia: **www.hayhouse.com.au**
Hay House South Africa: **www.hayhouse.co.za**
Hay House India: **www.hayhouse.co.in**

Supercoach

10 Secrets
to Transform
Anyone's Life

Michael Neill

HAY HOUSE

Australia • Canada • Hong Kong • India
South Africa • United Kingdom • United States

First published and distributed in the United Kingdom by:
Hay House UK Ltd, 292B Kensal Rd, London W10 5BE. Tel.: (44) 20
8962 1230; Fax: (44) 20 8962 1239. www.hayhouse.co.uk

Published and distributed in the United States of America by:
Hay House, Inc., PO Box 5100, Carlsbad, CA 92018-5100. Tel.: (1) 760
431 7695 or (800) 654 5126; Fax: (1) 760 431 6948 or (800) 650 5115.
www.hayhouse.com

Published and distributed in Australia by:
Hay House Australia Ltd, 18/36 Ralph St, Alexandria NSW 2015. Tel.:
(61) 2 9669 4299; Fax: (61) 2 9669 4144. www.hayhouse.com.au

Published and distributed in the Republic of South Africa by:
Hay House SA (Pty), Ltd, PO Box 990, Witkoppen 2068. Tel./Fax: (27)
11 467 8904. www.hayhouse.co.za

Published and distributed in India by:
Hay House Publishers India, Muskaan Complex, Plot No.3, B-2,
Vasant Kunj, New Delhi – 110 070. Tel.: (91) 11 4176 1620; Fax: (91)
11 4176 1630. www.hayhouse.co.in

Distributed in Canada by:
Raincoast, 9050 Shaughnessy St, Vancouver, BC V6P 6E5. Tel.: (1) 604
323 7100; Fax: (1) 604 323 2600

Copyright © 2009 by Michael Neill

Design: Bryn Starr Best

A version of the *West Side Story* text on page 5 was first published in
Spirit&Destiny Soul Secrets (Hay House UK, 2006).

The moral rights of the author have been asserted.

The information given in this book should not be treated as a
substitute for professional medical advice; always consult a medical
practitioner. Any use of information in this book is at the reader's
discretion and risk. Neither the author nor the publisher can be held
responsible for any loss, claim or damage arising out of the use, or
misuse, or the suggestions made or the failure to take medical advice.

Editor's note: In order to avoid awkward "he/she," "him/her"
references, the plural "they" or "their" has often been used to refer to
singular antecedents such as "person" or "partner" even though this
construction doesn't adhere to strict grammatical rules.

A catalogue record for this book is available from the British Library.

ISBN 978-1-78180-018-8

Printed and bound in Great Britain by TJ International Ltd.

To all the supercoaches, past and present, who have contributed their time, energy, love, and wisdom to creating a happier world.

"The only real voyage of discovery . . . consists not in seeking new landscapes but in having new eyes."

— **Marcel Proust**

CONTENTS

INTRODUCTION

A Different Way to Succeed

What if, regardless of your past history or the current economy, your dreams really could still come true?

What would you be most excited about having happen in your life over the next few weeks, months, or years? Would you like to experience dramatic breakthroughs in your career, business, or finances? Deeper love and connection with your family and intimate relationships? How about seemingly miraculous improvements in your own levels of health and well-being?

For the past 20 years or so, I've been a professional success coach—someone who gets paid to help make people's dreams come true. In that time, I've learned that not only are there many different types of dreams, there are also all sorts of different ways to reach them.

Whether you want to make more money, build your business, start a family, or save the world, chances are that your approach up until now has been primarily *practical*— that is, focused on what it is you want and what it is you think you need to do in order to make it happen.

If you're a reasonably progressive thinker, you're probably also aware that one of the reasons you want what you want is that you believe it will in some way enhance your *experience* of being alive. But as you may have already begun to realize, if you really want to have a more enjoyable life, reaching your goals is not enough. You're also going to have to find a more enjoyable way of getting there.

This is a book about succeeding from the inside out. When you learn to live your life in this way, stress disappears and worry becomes almost nonexistent. You realize that you were born happy and the worst thing that can ever happen to you is a thought—generally speaking, a thought about whatever you think is the worst thing that could ever happen to you. Things still won't always work out as you'd hoped or planned, but that just becomes a fact of life, instead of a problem to be solved. And since you live in a state of being full (of life, joy, love, and peace), going outside yourself to "find fulfillment" loses most of its appeal.

Of course, that doesn't mean you won't still do all sorts of weird and wonderful things with your life. It just means that you'll be using what's inside you to create things on the outside instead of doing them the other way around.

So how can a coach help?

The Three Levels of Change

"All miracles involve a shift in perception."

— *A Course in Miracles*

Traditional coaching takes place primarily on a horizontal dimension—coaches assist their clients in getting from point A to point B. Yet lasting, sustainable change nearly always happens in the vertical dimension—

a deepening of the ground of being of the client and greater access to inspiration and spiritual wisdom. While this has generally led to an either-or approach to success and personal growth and a sharp division between therapy and coaching, *transformative coaching* (or, as I like to call it, "supercoaching") uses the vertical dimensions to create change on the inside while you continue to move forward toward your goals on the outside.

The kinds of "vertical" changes that transformative coaching leads to can be usefully viewed on three levels. . . .

Level I: Change in a Specific Situation

Often people will hire a coach (or go to a counselor, therapist, or friend) to get help with a specific situation they're struggling with. They may want to deal with a difficult person at work, succeed at an important negotiation or job interview, or stay motivated as they train to beat their personal best at a sporting event.

This kind of "performance coaching" has long been a staple of the industry, and long before "life coaching" and "executive coaching" became common terms, people were using coaches in this capacity to help change their points of view, states of mind, or actions. At this level, people go from fear to confidence, from unease to comfort, or from inaction to action.

The impact of this kind of coaching is generally project specific. Once the difficult person has been handled, the interview completed, or the race run, people get on with the rest of their lives in much the same way they did before.

Level II: Change in a Specific Life Area

Sometimes we're less concerned with a specific event than we are with a whole category of events. This is why we find coaches specializing in any number of life areas: relationships, sales, parenting, confidence, presentations . . . the list goes on and on. People hire these experts to help them develop their confidence and increase their skills in whatever area they may be having difficulty. Like performance coaches, these coaches will help with specific situations, but they tend to measure their impact not just by how one situation changes, but by how their whole category of situations changes.

Level III: Global Change

The ultimate level of change is transformation, or what I sometimes call "global change"—a pervasive shift in our way of being in the world. At this level, it's not enough for us to develop a skill or change a feeling. It's our intangible "selves" we want to change, and in so doing, we change our experience of everything.

Each of the three levels maps across to a certain kind of intervention. When we want to make a change in the moment or in a specific situation, we apply a technique. When we want to make a change in a broader context, we install new strategies. But when we want to actually change *lives,* we need more than just strategies or techniques. We need a whole new paradigm or perspective—a new way of seeing.

So which level of change is best?

It depends. While Level III changes will ultimately make the biggest difference in people's lives, sometimes a smaller difference is all that's called for. For example, people heavily into personal development sometimes get fixated on finding Level III solutions for Level I problems—they've got a headache, but instead of taking an aspirin, they want to analyze the beliefs and lifestyle changes they need to make to become the kind of person who doesn't get headaches. It's not a bad idea, but it's a lot easier to do when your head isn't hurting!

The Three Levels in Action

Let's take an example. Bob is a customer service rep for a medium-sized manufacturing firm, and he's having a really bad day. When I ask him what his biggest sticking point is, he tells me it's a phone call he needs to make to a supplier in Detroit he's been having difficulties with.

If I were to intervene on Level I, I would probably work with his frame of mind by getting him into a more confident state. We might role-play a phone call with his supplier, and I would offer him tips and techniques to better handle the call and get the outcome he most wants. We might even choose to script the call, or at least the beginning of it, to help boost his confidence and resolve the situation.

But let's say I want more for Bob—I don't just want to assist him in getting through this one situation; I want to help turn him into a more effective employee, one who can handle a wider variety of customer service situations. At that point, I could give him books like

How to Talk So People Listen. I could teach him rapport skills like "matching and mirroring" so he could use body language to effectively allow others to feel more comfortable around him.

In time and with practice, Bob might well be able to turn things around and maybe even become the best customer service guy in the whole company. But in another way, nothing will have really changed. Because in order for something to change at a fundamental level, that change has to happen from the inside out.

At Level III, the coaching interventions are no longer about the supplier from Detroit or even about customer service. At Level III, we're dealing directly with Bob—the way he sees himself, the way he sees his job, and the way he sees other people. And when any one of those things changes, Bob will not only become more effective in his job, he'll also become more effective in his life.

Here's another example, one that might hit closer to home: Imagine you're having difficulties with your resident teenager. You want them to help out around the house and be more respectful toward you and your partner, but they seem determined to set a new world record for "most dirty clothes piled up in one corner of a bedroom."

At Level I, you could go in guns a-blazing and order them to pick up their dirty clothes "or else." You might even try a subtler approach—the dangling carrot of concert tickets or a shopping trip to the nearest mall in exchange for a cleaner room.

At Level II, you would read parenting books that would tell you how to handle discipline problems with teens, or even one on how to handle difficult people at work in the hopes that you could map it across to your own child at home. (Of course, if you come across a copy of *What to Do When You Work for an Idiot* in their bedroom, chances are they're planning a little Level II intervention with you!)

But at Level III, you would know that what's called for is a shift in perspective—a new way of seeing the situation.

For example, when my daughter Clara was six, she went through a period of violent temper tantrums that frightened her teachers to the point where they were considering either putting her on medication or kicking her out of school. My wife and I had no clue what to do about it, so we turned to one of my mentors, supercoach Bill Cumming.

He helped us by approaching the situation on all three levels simultaneously. At Level I, he would continually check in with us to ensure that we were doing okay within ourselves—that is, we were getting adequate sleep, food, and exercise and doing whatever else we needed for spiritual self-care.

At Level II, he taught us some wonderful strategies for dealing with difficult children. The one that sticks in my mind is the two C's: *clarity* and *consistency*. We got clear about what was and wasn't okay, and we were consistent in our enforcement of those rules.

However, what made the biggest difference, and has stayed with us to this day, was the Level III intervention. In working with Bill, we came to realize that the only reason someone would behave in the way Clara was behaving was if the person felt unwell within themselves. As we began to see the discomfort in Clara that was leading to her acting out, it became much easier not to take her behavior personally, as if it was her way of punishing us for our parenting failures.

More important, any catastrophizing we'd been doing in our heads about how this would be a problem for the rest of her life, and if it was this bad now, "imagine how bad it will be when she's a teenager," fell away. We began to see her as a little girl doing the best she could to control her environment, and knew that when she had better strategies at her disposal, her innate wisdom and common sense would guide her to use them. That made it easy and natural to feel the full force of our love for her, even when she was behaving in ways that were shocking and at times a little bit frightening for us. Instead of sending her to her room when she had a tantrum in a behaviorist effort to "extinguish" the unwanted behavior, I began to go into her room with her and just quietly be with her as she worked through whatever it was she was working through.

At first, she didn't seem to like our new approach. Instead of simply putting holes in the walls of her bedroom, she seemed hell-bent on putting a few in my head. But after a few tantrums, she somehow recognized that she was safe with us—and that feeling of safety allowed some protective mechanism inside her to let go and her natural wisdom to come back to the fore.

Now, six years later, Clara is more secure in herself and her thinking than most adults. And while we may well butt heads at some point during her teenage years, it's far more likely to be due to something triggered in us than in her!

Ten Sessions to Transform Your Life

> *"All people occasionally stumble across the truth,*
> *but most pick themselves up and continue*
> *as if nothing had happened."*

— attributed to Winston Churchill

This book is laid out in ten coaching sessions, each one built around a "secret" understanding about life. We could call these secrets "principles," in the sense that they will reliably guide us through the uncharted territory of life; we could also call them "understandings," in the sense that once we understand them, we'll never relate to our problems, goals, or the people in our lives in the same way again.

Each session is designed to be a catalyst—something that will spark your own insights about your work, your finances, your relationships, and yourself. An insight is something that once seen (by looking within, hence "in-sight") can never be *un*seen. That's why there's nothing here to master and no particular skills or techniques to learn.

This insight-based approach is another difference between Level I and II *change,* which often involves hard work and disciplined practice over time; and Level III *transformation,* which is seemingly effortless in its application yet profound in its effects.

What makes most change seem difficult is that we're trying to do it from the outside in—that is, to change our external behavior without making any change in how we're seeing the situation on the inside. Because there's no internal basis for making the change, we need external motivation, reminders, and any other threats and bribes we can think of in order to get us to consistently behave in the ways that we or someone else has decided are good for us. But the moment we see things differently, either because we have more information or we've had some kind of insight, change is natural and inevitable.

Let's imagine for a moment that you travel to work each weekday morning. And let's pretend that it's a fairly unpleasant commute—it takes upwards of an hour there and back, and there's either a lot of traffic at that time of day or the subway is inevitably packed, or both. Now, let's say I happen to know a shortcut you could take that would enable you to bend the laws of physics so you get to work and back in no more than five minutes. Better still, the journey would be pleasant, uncrowded, and rather beautiful. How many times would I have to show you the new route before you began taking it as a matter of course?

It wouldn't matter if you'd been doing things in the old way for years, or if you had low self-esteem or a difficult childhood. The moment you saw that this new route was a genuinely better way to get where you wanted to go, you'd begin to take it. The entire experience would be effortless, because the external change (your new behavior) would be the natural fruit of the internal change—your new understanding of what was possible.

In a similar way, each session in this book will enable you to see a number of "shortcuts" to happiness, success, and well-being. And as your understanding of what's possible grows, your life will begin to change for the better, all by itself.

How to Use This Book

> *"Don't cut the person to fit the cloth."*
>
> — Sufi saying

Perhaps the most effective way to use this book would be to read through it cover to cover, then go back and spend a week or so playing with the ideas in each session. But then again, perhaps not.

Each person is unique, and the value you'll get from reading this book will be found more in the insights it provokes than the actual content or exercises. In other words, you may get everything you need in one reading, but if you find yourself wanting more, it's designed to stand up to deeper inspection and introspection.

In these pages, I'll be sharing a few strategies and techniques that my clients and I have found effective in creating more and more wonderful lives. But by and large I'll be focusing on new perspectives—new ways of seeing that will lead to appreciating new possibilities and taking new actions in your life and the lives of the people you care about most.

At the beginning of each session, you'll find a story. These are written for a different part of your mind and are there simply to be enjoyed. Don't worry if you can't figure out why a particular story is at the beginning of a particular session—if it matters, the connection will come to you, and if it doesn't matter . . . well, it doesn't matter!

You'll also find two kinds of exercises throughout the text:

1. **Coaching exercises** are generally in the body of the text and are intended to be practiced and played with as you go through each session. They're designed to facilitate transformation, and often produce the kinds of Level III insights that lead to effortless success and change.

2. **Supercoaching tips** are bite-size versions of the techniques and strategies I use with my clients to help them break through whatever is holding them back from going wherever it is they want to go. Whether you're a helping professional, use coaching as a part of your job, or simply want to be able to make more of a difference in your own life and the lives of your family and friends, these tips will serve you well!

Creating Effortless Success

One of the best descriptions of the shift that happens when you begin to live your life from a deeper understanding of these secrets is the creation of what my clients and I call "effortless success." This isn't about an avoidance of physical effort; it's about an absence of mental struggle. Happiness leads to success, well-being leads to inspiration, and that success and inspiration become the basis for creating an ever more wonderful life.

In my work with private clients and discussions with readers and students, I've come to recognize that the journey to effortless success takes people through three distinct stages of development. While the length of time it takes a person to go through each of these stages varies wildly, the stages themselves appear to be quite consistent. . . .

Stage 1: Learning a New Way to Drive

Some years ago, I interviewed supercoach Maria Nemeth, and she shared the following analogy for what it's like when she meets a new client for the first time:

> Imagine a person standing in front of you complaining they can't walk properly because of a sore foot. As they're calling your attention toward their foot, you can't help noticing that they're holding a gun directly above it, pointing straight down.
>
> Next, you notice they have a severe twitch every couple of minutes and that every time they twitch, the gun goes off, sending another bullet directly into their foot.
>
> No matter how enthusiastic and motivated they are to begin moving forward, it would be a waste of time to work on getting anywhere, or even on healing their wounded foot, until you did something about the gun and the twitch.

Similarly, when I begin work with a new client, they often come to me with a list of goals they want to get started on immediately. Yet inevitably our first few sessions together are spent clearing up loose ends in their lives and building a foundation that will ultimately support their dreams.

The general report from people in this phase is that a sense of ease and well-being begins to permeate their lives, coupled with a sense of surprise that things have begun to shift in their circumstances "all by themselves." This can be unsettling! As one client said to me with great concern in his voice, "The problem is, I don't have any more problems."

When you're in this stage, you may find yourself worrying about not being worried, and being a bit upset about the fact that nothing seems to upset you anymore. As another client told me, "It feels like something is missing from my life." When we explored this statement further, it turned out that what was missing was all the stress!

While for some people the relief of reaching this kind of equanimity is success enough, I'm interested in complete transformation. Some of my clients were already pretty far down the road to success when they first hired me, but after a while it's as though they've learned to drive in a whole new way. That's why for me peace of mind and greater contentment and happiness aren't the end of the road but the place where the journey really begins. . . .

Stage 2: Driving Daddy's Ferrari

When people first learn the principles of creating effortless, happy success and begin to put them into practice, the results they produce (and the way in which they produce them) can be quite startling. Customers and clients appear out of nowhere. Business opportunities show up "out of the blue." Relationship miracles occur, and seemingly insurmountable problems simply dissolve without ever being addressed directly.

At this stage, people often go back and forth between being thrilled with the way that their lives are unfolding and terrified that "the magic will stop working" and they'll go right back to how things were before we started.

One day a client explained this feeling to me by saying, "It's like I'm driving my daddy's Ferrari—it's incredibly fun, and I'm really moving forward, but every time I start to feel that I'm going too fast, I slam on the brakes because I'm terrified of crashing the car!"

My explanation for this is simple:

Traditional success models are all about <u>doing</u>;
creating effortless success is all about <u>being</u>.

It's easy to track the cause and effect with a doing-based model—the more you do, the better the result. But in creating effortless success, you do less and achieve more. People often get uncomfortable in this stage because they haven't yet seen the connection between how they're being in the world and the results they're producing.

Amazing things happen at first, but the results begin to diminish over time. It seems as though things aren't working as well as they used to, or that the "magic" only works on the small stuff.

In some cases, the discomfort can get so, well, *uncomfortable* that people would rather go back to doing things the way they used to. Even though it's harder and less sustainable, at least it makes sense to them—at least they feel they have some control.

But for those people who stick with it, there's a third stage—the most wonderful stage of all. . . .

Stage 3: Owning the Garage

At some point, people understand that creating effortless success isn't magic (although it certainly is magical)—it's the natural result of approaching life from a place of profound well-being, listening for the inner call, and following it wherever it may lead.

In this stage, you realize it's not your daddy's Ferrari; it's *yours*—and that it's just one of the wonderful cars you have in your garage. There's no fear that "it will stop working" because you realize that "it" never worked—the power to create the life you wanted to live was inside you right from the very beginning.

What seems to facilitate this transition is a new level of understanding of how it all works—an insight or series of insights into what's really going on. And whether that understanding is triggered by a coach, a book, a seminar, or even a casual comment by a friend, once you really see it, you can never lose it. Because the realization comes from inside you, it's yours to keep.

So let's look directly at you for a moment. Which stage of development does it seem like you're currently at?

Are you:

- Struggling to move forward? Moving forward by struggling? *(Stage 1)*

- Experiencing wonderful results and even seeming miracles but secretly wondering when the magic is going to stop, when the batteries are going to run out, or how you'll ever be able to apply this to "the big stuff" in your life? *(Stage 2)*

- Living life as a creator, at peace in yourself (mostly!) and knowing that you have the power within you to create whatever it is you most want to see in the world? *(Stage 3)*

Wherever you currently are, you can use the ten sessions in this book to assist with your transition—either from struggle to ease or from ease to peace. As you set your direction, stay with your good feelings, and listen for the whispers of wisdom, you'll be amazed by how easy that transition will be.

Your journey begins just as soon as you turn this page. . . .

The Art and Science
of Make-Believe

"'There's no use trying,' said Alice:
'one can't believe impossible things.'
'I daresay you haven't had much practice,' said the Queen.
'When I was your age, I always did it for half an hour
a day. Why, sometimes I've believed as many as six
impossible things before breakfast.'"

— from *Alice's Adventures in Wonderland,*
by Lewis Carroll

The Lion and the Fox

A man was walking through the woods outside his home one day when he came across a hungry fox who seemed to be at death's door. Because he was a kind man, he thought to bring it some food, but before he could go back to his home, he heard a fearsome roar and hid behind a tree. In seconds, a mountain lion appeared, dragging the carcass of its freshly caught prey. The lion ate its fill and then wandered off, leaving the remains for the grateful fox.

The man was overwhelmed by this example of an abundant and benevolent universe and decided that he wouldn't return to his home or his job. Instead of working hard to provide for himself, he would follow the example of the fox and allow the universe to provide for him.

Needless to say, the fox wandered off, and as days turned to weeks, the man himself was hungry and at death's door. Despite his best efforts to retain his faith, he was becoming desperate. In a rare moment of inner quiet, he heard the still, small voice of his own wisdom: "Why have you sought to emulate the fox instead of the lion?"

With that, the man returned home and ate his fill.

◆

The Power of Make-Believe

I began acting when I was 6 years old; at the age of 12, I played Hamlet. But the experience that really launched my quest for understanding the human psyche didn't come until I was 15. I was playing Pepe, one of the Puerto Rican gang members, in a youth-theater production of *West Side Story.*

Now there's a musical number fairly early on in the show called "Dance at the Gym." And this was the first chance we Puerto Ricans really got to strut our stuff. The choreography was sexy, very Latin, and noisy—lots of shouting of *"Ay, Caramba"* and *"Chee, Chee, Chee"* and other approximations of what a bunch of small-town white kids imagined Puerto Rican gang members would say.

This was my favorite part of the show, and this particular night we really got into it. We danced until the sweat was pouring, and the lights were hot and the girls were hot and the music was hot and it felt like the whole theater was burning up.

We were all riding that passion and feeling those really intense feelings, and then we got into the scene called the Rumble. Well, we'd done this dozens of times before. The Americans taunted us; we taunted them; there was a lot of macho dancing (this time with switchblades); and in the end, Bernardo stabbed Riff and we all ran like hell. Only this time, something different happened.

One of the American gang members, a big blond guy named Snowball, was looking at me, and he started calling out, *"Ay, Caramba"* and *"Chee, Chee, Chee,"* and making fun of the way we'd been dancing in the previous scene. And all of a sudden I went from hot to furious. Not pretend, not acting—genuinely furious.

Now I don't know if you've ever been made fun of for your race, appearance, gender, or sexuality, but I was so filled with anger at that moment that I wanted to leap across the stage and kill him.

Fortunately for both of us, there was a curious part of me that was observing the whole scene and offered up some useful counterarguments. First, I'm not Puerto Rican. Second, the actor playing Snowball was actually a good friend I hung out with offstage. Third, we weren't on the mean streets of New York City—we were in a theater in a small town in Massachusetts, doing a play in front of a few hundred people.

Yet the anger I felt when the person *he* was pretending to be insulted the person *I* was pretending to be was red-hot and real.

What I came to realize that night is that if you "make believe" something long enough (like being a Puerto Rican gang member), it becomes real to you—you begin to think and feel and act as if it's really true. Otherwise I would never have been upset about being teased for being Puerto Rican. (Let's face it, assuming you're not one, if someone called you a "stupid tuna fish" you probably wouldn't take it personally.)

What do you believe right now? Take a few moments to finish these "sentence starters" for yourself. You can do this in your head, but I strongly encourage you to jot down your answers in the space on the next page. That's because they're likely to have changed so radically by the time we've finished our time together that you won't remember them later.

- Life is ...
- I am ...
- People are ...
- Money is ...
- The most important thing to know about happiness is ...

Now, however you've finished those sentences —positive or negative, thought-through or impulsive, heartfelt or not—is simply an insight into how you currently see the world. Hopefully, you chose to answer honestly, knowing that no one but you need ever see your answers.

Look again at your answers. Do they feel "right" to you? Can you think of lots of evidence and examples to back them up?

The secret we'll be exploring in this session underpins everything else we'll be doing together, because it explains why we see what we see, hear what we hear, feel what we feel, and do what we do. It's a secret that has been talked about in many eras and many traditions from around the world and is "secret" not because no one wants you to know it, but because it's so difficult to talk about—like trying to explain the concept of water to a fish.

The secret is that we each live in our own separate reality. This isn't some kind of an esoteric theory, but a physiological fact. Our brains filter information through the five senses, then make representations of that information inside our minds. We then experience these representations, first as thoughts and then as emotions.

But as we represent the information in our minds, certain bits of the data are inevitably deleted, distorted, and generalized. And since we all delete, distort, and generalize that information slightly differently, we all have slightly (or sometimes completely) different perceptions of what is going on around us.

In other words, the way we think determines what we see, hear, and feel, regardless of what's actually going on around us in the world. Or, to put it slightly differently, there's what happens, and there's what we think about what happens. And what makes this important is that the lion's share of our decisions, feelings, and actions in life will be based on our thoughts, not the objective facts.

This is neither a new idea nor one associated with any particular field of study. In quantum physics, the uncertainty principle says that we can never study anything objectively because "the observer always influences the observed." Psychologists talk about "the Pygmalion effect," and linguists say, "The map is not the territory." Shakespeare wrote that "there is nothing either good or bad, but thinking makes it so," and the Bible says, "For as [a man] thinketh in his heart, so is he."

Perhaps my favorite way of thinking about this secret comes from one of my early mentors, author and supercoach Serge Kahili King. He describes the principle of thought like this:

The world is what you think it is.

While at first glance this may seem like an innocuous idea, its implications are far-reaching. If the world is what you think it is, then life becomes one giant self-fulfilling prophecy. Your expectations create your experience, and if anything happens that confounds your expectations, you will most likely find a way of explaining it away or fitting it into your existing worldview. And any attempt you might make to "prove" your theories about the world objectively will never gain universal acceptance, because you're creating that world through your thinking in one way, and other people are creating it through their thinking in another.

If this all seems much too heady for a book about having more happiness, ease, and success in your life, here's a simple experiment to experience this phenomenon for yourself:

1. Get a piece of paper and a pen.

2. Now, take 30 seconds to look around you and make a list of everything you can see that's green. (Do this before you move on to Step 3.)

3. When you've completed your list, put down your pen. As soon as you finish reading this sentence, close your eyes and make a list of everything around you that's brown.

Now, if you actually took the minute or so it takes to do this experiment, you will have had a direct experience of the effect what you hold in your mind has on what you experience in the world. If you're still a bit befuddled, all you need to remember is this:

**You'll always tend to see whatever
it is you're looking for.**

Everything you'll be learning in our time together is based on the fact that you're creating your experience of *everything* in your life through the way that you think about it. If you're having a wonderful experience, well done—you're creating that experience from the raw material of your life. If you're having a horrible experience, well, well done—you're creating that, and it can begin to change at any moment. Because once you really begin to understand how your thoughts create your "reality," you'll no longer be a victim of the process.

Plato's Cave for a New Millennium

Imagine you're sitting in a theater watching a scary movie. The movie is well made, and you get caught up in it to the point where you physically shrink back into your seat when the pretty girl heads down the dark stairway with an old flashlight whose batteries mysteriously stop working as soon as she hears a strange creaking sound from the farthest, darkest corner of the basement. As the music builds toward a crescendo and you just know a monster is going to burst forth at any moment . . . someone's cell phone goes off, repeatedly playing the opening bars of that pop song you can never get out of your head no matter how hard you try.

From this moment forward, regardless of how gripped you've been by the movie, it will be difficult to get back into it in the same way.

Now let's watch another movie together. This is a movie about *you*. It's filled with problems and obstacles and triumphs and tragedies. It's a movie where you see yourself failing to achieve what you want to achieve, being dragged down again and again by your tragic personal history, or succeeding against the odds and triumphing in the end. It's a movie about how difficult it is to find true love, or how lucky you are to have found it for yourself; how men and women are sinners or saints; and how people always mean well or stab you in the back every time. Whether you're stuck in a cubicle or living large in a corner office, working from home or not working at all, this is the movie of your life—for better or worse, in sickness and in health, for richer or poorer.

This time, instead of a cell phone going off, I'm going to ask you to turn your attention away from the screen and come with me back up into the projection booth. But before we do that, let's talk a little bit about the principles of creation.

The Principles of Creation

Any painter, in order to become more effective at creating art, needs to understand the basic principles of painting—color, texture, perspective, and line. Of course, simply understanding them will probably not cause your next painting to be a universally acclaimed masterpiece, but it will make it far more likely that your work will become better and better and you'll find more and more joy in its creation.

In the same way, if you want to be more effective at creating your life, it's important to understand the principles behind that creation.

In order to create any experience, three elements need to be present:

1. **Energy.** Without some sort of raw material to create from, there can be no creation. Fortunately for us, physicists have already demonstrated that everything we can see, hear, feel, taste, or touch is made up of the same source energy. Rocks are made up of the same energy as sound, and both are made up of the same energy as you and me.

Long before Einstein ever realized that $E = mc^2$, philosophers theorized about the underlying nature of the universe, prophets talked about everything being a part of God, and mystics meditated on all things emerging from the primordial soup.

Regardless of whether you use scientific or spiritual language to describe it, this energy is the source and substance of all things bright and beautiful, all creatures great and small.

2. **Consciousness.** What allows us to make different-iations between ourselves and others in this "spiritual soup" is our individual consciousness—the ability we all have to experience our own separate version of the unchanging whole. Without light, we wouldn't be able to experience the beauty of a sunset (or even a picture of a sunset); without sound, we couldn't hear the birds twittering in the morning or our friends twittering in the next room. In the same way, it is our consciousness—literally our ability to be consciously aware of something—that allows us to experience whatever it is we're experiencing in our lives.

3. **Thought.** If source energy is the paint, thought is the paintbrush. Our life is the canvas, and our consciousness is what allows us to appreciate the painting. Because different

thoughts come in and out of our heads throughout the day, our experience is continually changing. But because we tend to focus on the same limited range of thoughts throughout the day, there is a sense of cohesive reality to our experience.

Of course, just because a thought pops into your head doesn't mean it will immediately manifest in your life. (If it did, there would be more deaths by roller coasters going off their tracks, people falling from very high places, and heads exploding due to stress than any other cause.) That's because in and of themselves, thoughts have no power. It's only when you invest your own energy and consciousness into them that they begin to become real. A thought without your personal investment is no more powerful than a tea bag without boiling water. It's only after you add the water that the tea begins to infuse and create the flavor, and it's only after you add your agreement and energy to a thought that it begins to impact your life.

What makes thoughts *appear* to be so powerful is that the more we invest our energy into them, the more "real" they start to feel.

(This is why positive thinking so often backfires—it energizes negative thoughts by making them into "things" that must be avoided. Simply noticing your negative thoughts arising and allowing them to fade away will nearly always work better than bringing in the thought police to try to control them.)

So to review, there are three things necessary in order to experience anything:

1. There needs to be a ground of being—I'm calling that energy, but you could just as easily call it "spirit" or "source," or even "Jethro," and it would work just the same.

2. There needs to be a creative force—in this case, thought.

3. There needs to be a way of experiencing and understanding all that is happening—our current level of consciousness.

Our formula is now clear:

Energy + Consciousness + Thought = Creation

Let's go back to the projection booth. . . .

Whatever is happening on the screen is your experience of life. What's being projected onto that screen will appear real to you to the extent that it fits with the movie you're used to seeing.

The projector is your consciousness—it simply shines the bright white light of awareness on whatever is projected in front of it. If that light isn't on (i.e., if you're "unconscious"), you'll have no awareness of and no direct experience of your thoughts.

Each reel of film running in front of the projector is made up of your thoughts. If you have scary thoughts, you'll see scary things on the screen of your experience and experience scary feelings; if you're projecting romantic thoughts, you'll see romantic things on the screen and tend to feel romantic feelings in your heart. Comedies will usually make you laugh and tragedies make you cry—that's just the way things work.

What powers it all? The electricity behind life—the underlying energy of the universe. (We could just as easily say the whole movie theater is made up of energy as well, but let's save that conversation for another time!)

Why does all this matter? Because if you're watching a film you don't really enjoy, you're unlikely to try to change it by getting into a prolonged debate with the characters on the screen about it. If you do, you probably don't expect them to respond in turn.

But when it comes to the movie of our lives, the first place most of us go to change things is right up to the screen. We spend all our time and money and energy trying to change our experience on the outside, not realizing that the whole thing is being projected from the inside out.

So how do we change things if we don't like the movie? By making up a different one!

I've been a student of thought and the art and science of make-believe since that performance of *West Side Story* all those years ago, and here are two of the most important things I've learned:

1. **What you believe tends to become true for you.** Unlike road maps, which must accurately reflect the territory they describe in order to be of use, our mental maps actually re-create the territory as they're describing it. Since these maps often become self-fulfilling prophecies, we can change our experience of the world (and ultimately the world itself) by changing the way we choose to see it.

In other words:

Over time, the map becomes the territory.

If you see the world as a friendly place, you'll tend to notice the ways in which things work out for the best. Because you're looking for "friendly" things to happen, you're that much more likely to find them. At times, you may even create them with your intention and your actions.

2. **You can make believe anything**. In order to make believe something is true, you simply tell yourself that it's true, collect evidence that supports your story, and then act accordingly. In this way it's possible to make believe absolutely anything. (If you find this difficult to believe, look up the cautionary tale of Marian Keech or the modern-day Flat Earth Society.)

So, instead of always trying to align your beliefs with "reality," it's possible to align your beliefs with what you most want to create in your life. And when you consistently make believe in what you want, you can begin to create some pretty unbelievable results!

Here's a Level I coaching exercise that can lead to some wonderful Level III insights. . . .

Changing the Movie of Your Life

1. Write down your top three goals in any area of your life.

2. For each one, write out some things that it would be useful to "make believe" were true. For example:

Goal: "To be the top-performing salesperson at my company."

Make-believes:

- "Selling is easy and fun for me."
- "The more people I speak with, the easier it is for me to sell."
- "Learning to sell will make me a more spiritual person."

Goal: "To be blissfully married to the perfect person for me."

Make-believes:

- "There are a number of people who could be the perfect person for me."
- "I am a great catch!"
- "The more I am attracted to others, the more attractive I will be to them."

Remember, the idea here isn't to find what you currently believe to be true, just anything you think would be useful if you *did* believe it.

3. Actively make believe what you want by doing any or all of the following exercises:

a. *Tell yourself that it's true.* You can accelerate the effect of this by simply repeating the statement again and again in a physiology of certainty. To do this, tell yourself something you know to be true—for instance, "Today is ____, and my name is ____," and then repeat your new make-believe in exactly the same tone of voice and holding your body in exactly the same way. It may take a few tries (or even a few hundred!), but when you can totally match the voice tone and physiology, you'll notice your new make-believe actually "feels" truer.

b. *Gather evidence that it's true.* Plug each make-believe on your list into the following format and fill in the blanks as many times as you can:

"I know this is true for me because ____;
for example, ____."

Here's an example:

Make-believe: "The more I am attracted to others, the more attractive I will be to them."

- "I know this is true for me because I am always more attracted to people when they're 'lit from within'; for example, the way that girl looked so beautiful when she smiled at her boyfriend at the restaurant the other day."

c. *Act as if it's true.* Ask yourself: "If I knew [*the new make-believe*], what would I do to get what I wanted?"

For example:

- "If I knew that learning to sell would make me a more spiritual person, what would I do to become the top-performing salesperson at my company?"
- "If I knew that I was a great catch, what would I do to find the perfect person for me?"

4. When you've come up with a list of actions, choose at least one to take in the next 24 hours.

No Complaints

Since complaining is the opposite of creation, one task I often give my clients when we first start working together is to put them on a "complaint fast"—that is, I ask them to go a day or a week or a month deliberately not complaining (out loud!) about anything.

That's not to say that if they order pizza for lunch and the waiter brings them a hamburger, they shouldn't send it back. It just means that they don't follow that up with a list of complaints to the waiter, their friends, the manager of the restaurant, and the editorial page of the local paper about what an awful place the world has become when decent hardworking folk can't even get a slice of pizza without having to deal with gross incompetence and a possible case of criminal negligence!

To create a "complaint fast" for yourself, resolve to go one week without complaining. If you complain even once during that week (and you almost certainly will), begin again with day one.

It took me the better part of a year to complete the experiment for the first time myself, but the resulting change is incredibly worthwhile!

From Victim to Creator

Have you ever been in a stressful situation? Seen a powerful movie? Read a sad novel or an inspiring book?

I can guarantee that you haven't, because each one of those qualities—stress, power, sadness, and inspiration—are actually inside you, not part of the event you're attributing them to. You're the one experiencing the stress, power, sadness, and inspiration; and in fact, biochemically speaking, you're even the one creating them.

Why does this matter?

Because when you act as if your experience is created from the outside in, you will experience yourself as a victim. The minute you take responsibility for creating your experience from the inside out, you reclaim your position as the creator of your life.

Here's an example from one of my clients, a property developer I'll call Fred for the purposes of this illustration.

Fred was what I call a "successful victim." He had all sorts of wonderful things in his life, but because he had no idea that he was creating his own experience, he lived in constant fear of everything being taken away from him. Although he made a lot of money by most people's standards, he never felt that he had enough.

When I asked him to tell me some of his thoughts about money, he explained with great seriousness, "Making money is hard, managing money is stressful, and losing money would be terrifying." His goal for our coaching was for me to help him make a lot more money so he wouldn't have to worry about it anymore.

I shared the inside-out distinction with him and asked him to rephrase his statements, this time taking responsibility for his experience of money.

Here's what he came up with:

- "I find it hard to make money."
- "I find it stressful to manage money."
- "I find the thought of losing money terrifying."

Just for fun, I asked him to take it a step further and to truly think of himself as the creator of his experience. In addition, I pointed out that just as our thoughts are always changing, our experience of things is rarely constant, although we often describe it as if it were.

Here was his third iteration:

- "I often create the experience of difficulty when I do what I do to make money."
- "I often stress myself out when I think about managing my money."
- "I often terrify myself by thinking about losing what I have and projecting into the future."

This then gave us our new goals for him to work on in our coaching:

1. To experience more ease and well-being in his work

2. To experience happiness and well-being while managing his money

3. To motivate himself to make smart financial

decisions by inspiring himself instead of terrifying himself

4. To experience himself as the owner of his life and creator of his experience, capable of creating pleasure, satisfaction, and meaning in everything he did

Not only was he able to transform his experience around money over the course of the first few months, but within a year he was making more, worrying less, and in his words, "creating a wonderful experience of being alive."

Whose Life Is It Anyway?

1. Write a paragraph or two about a situation or area of your life where you would like things to be different. For example:

> "My relationship is just awful. I thought I'd found myself a great guy, but I obviously got that one wrong—he's obsessive and moody and impossible to spend time around."

2. Go back through what you've written and circle any phrases where you've attributed qualities of being (stress, ease, difficulty, fear, and so on) to other people or external events.

3. Rewrite your story as if those qualities are things you bring to your experience, not ones that you get from it. If you like, take into account that most experiences are temporary and changeable. For example:

> "I'm really not enjoying my relationship with Tony at the moment. I like a lot of things about him, but I find it difficult to cope when he seems to be up in his head instead of fully present with me."

4. Just for fun, rewrite your story as if you were truly the creator of your experience. What would be your goals/intentions for creating more of what you wanted? For example:

> "Whenever I see Tony frowning or ask him a question and only get a grunt in response, I go up into my head and create nightmare scenarios of how awful this will be in 20 years' time. I make myself really sad and angry, hoping that if I can just get angry enough, I'll find the courage to either talk to him about it or move on with my life. . . . What I really want is to feel happy inside myself regardless of what's going on with Tony, and to be there for him if he wants me to be. If he really doesn't want to change, I want to feel ready and able to move on."

In a nutshell:

- The world is what you think it is.

- You'll always tend to see whatever it is you're looking for.

- You're creating your experience of life right now, moment by moment.

If you like, you can take some time to just live with what we've been discussing before moving on. Reread it as often as you like, play with it, do the exercises, and give yourself some space to notice the changes that will begin to happen "all by themselves." No rush—you've got all the time in the world!

Have fun, learn heaps, and when you're ready, I'll join you in the next session. . . .

SESSION TWO

You Were Born Happy

"The fact that millions of people share the same forms of mental pathology does not make these people sane."

— Erich Fromm

An Old Sioux Legend

In ancient times, the Creator wanted to hide something from the humans until they were ready to see it. He gathered all the other creatures of creation to ask for their advice.

The eagle said, "Give it to me and I will take it to the highest mountain in all the land," but the Creator said, "No, one day they will conquer the mountain and find it."

The salmon said, "Leave it with me and I will hide it at the very bottom of the ocean," but the Creator said, "No, for humans are explorers at heart, and one day they will go there, too."

The buffalo said, "I will take it and bury it in the very heart of the great plains," but the Creator said, "No, for one day even the skin of the earth will be ripped open, and they will find it there."

The creatures of creation were stumped, but then an old blind mole spoke up. "Why don't you put it inside them—that's the very last place they'll look."

The Creator said, "It is done."

◆

The Essence of Essence

Recently, a woman whose thoughts were in a terrible spin called in to my radio show. She was worried about everything and trying to solve all her problems at once. I interrupted her litany of woes and asked her what I'm sure she thought was a complete non sequitur.

"If you had a bowl of murky water and you wanted to make that water clear," I said, "what would you do?"

She thought for a moment and then suggested boiling it.

I laughed because I recognized that this was exactly what she was doing with her own thoughts. She was attempting to gain clarity by trying harder than ever to figure everything out. As a strategy, this is like increasing traffic to reduce pollution, turning up the volume to drown out the noise, or attempting to bomb your way to a peaceful resolution. It's not that these strategies have never been attempted; it's just that they hardly ever work.

If you want to make murky water clear, you have to leave it alone long enough for the murk to settle. The reason this works is because the nature of water is clear. The nature of the mind is clear, too, and the nature of a human being is well.

When I studied a few years back with supercoaches Gay and Kathlyn Hendricks, they shared a distinction with me they called "essence" and "persona."

At the level of essence, there are no boundaries—we are all one. Deep inside, we all want the same things: to love and be loved, to care and be cared for, and to live as happily as we can in whatever world we've been born into. In times of crisis, this common humanity tends to come to the fore, which is why we'll often come across acts of incredible kindness, understanding, and compassion in the face of great tragedy.

One Minute for Yourself

The next time you're speaking or working with someone and the person seems stuck, suggest that you both take exactly one minute to do whatever you can do and/or need to do to become fully present to the moment.

You'll both be amazed by how much your energy shifts!

Exploring essence is a lifetime pursuit and is the endgame of a number of spiritual traditions and practices. But most of us get so caught up in the game of persona that we miss out on the joy and wisdom that are an ever-deepening presence at the level of our essential selves.

The Birth of Persona

I recently watched the somewhat laughable 1950s romantic drama *Scaramouche* starring Stewart Granger and Janet Leigh. In the movie, a hideously scarred actor has been making his living playing a masked romantic clown by the name of Scaramouche. At some point, unbeknownst to the local police, his mask is taken over by a handsome political radical played by Granger.

Granger is able to function right under the noses of the local police because they believe they know all about the hideous creature that lives beneath the mask. In the same way, most of us have spent so long pretending to be whatever it is we're pretending to be that any pretense of living from our true selves is long gone. We begin to make up a new story, one based on our underlying awareness that we're not who we appear to be—that at any moment, we'll be unmasked and found out as the phonies and frauds that we are. The more energy we put into developing our mask, the more convinced we become that we really need one.

Unlike essence, which is something we're all born with, our personas are created and maintained throughout our lives. At first, they develop as a kind of unconscious reaction to what is going on in the world around us.

To better understand this, imagine yourself inside a "motel womb." You've been there for around nine months, so you're feeling completely at home, although lately things have been a bit cramped. You're relaxing on your heated waterbed, snacking on placenta-flavored potato chips, minding your own business, when all of a sudden—*boom!*—you feel an earthquake start to shake the bed. Before you know it, you're being pushed out through the door by an unseen force with the intensity of a tornado. You stumble out into the blinding light, get smacked on the behind by a masked giant, and begin to scream.

It's hardly surprising at this point that the desire for safety might arise. And feeling safe and well is a wonderful thing. But that initial experience of danger is so profound that it can continue to be triggered throughout our lives, and we begin to crave "security"—the knowledge that not only are we safe now, but that we'll always be safe. Whenever we feel *un*safe, we seek to control our environment and particularly the people around us in order to return to safety. Now, some of these people will allow us to "control" them through the intensity of our feelings, especially if through our anger or sadness or fear, we're able to stimulate their own insecurity and desire to be safe. But sooner or later we come to the realization that we can't control everyone.

However, even if we can't control people, we soon work out that we can still stay safe around them.

How?

Well, it turns out that if people approve of what we're doing, they won't hurt us (most of the time). So we learn to be "nice" and to do as we're told so that "they" approve of us and we get to stay safe—at least for as long as they keep approving of us.

In doing so, we begin to develop a persona—an act—that will fool all those scary giants out there into believing that we're actually the way they want us to be. The problem comes when we forget that it's just an act—when we start to believe that we actually are who we've been pretending to be.

As a friend of mine once put it, we're like diamonds who have spent so much time applying layer upon layer of nail polish to appear beautiful to the world that we begin to believe we must be covered in horse crap.

Most coaching—certainly at Level I and Level II—is focused on finding better ways to apply the nail polish. Most therapy is spent digging through the horse crap. But the "supercoach approach" is to look inside and discover the diamond within.

The Source of Well-being

People often live as though their experience of life takes place on a continuum ranging from misery to joy.

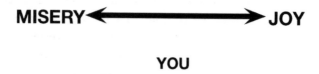

The game of life then becomes about figuring out how to spend more time at the happy end of the continuum and less time at the miserable end.

At one level of consciousness, this path toward greater happiness seems to be marked by having the right stuff—plenty of money, a good job, a great relationship, and a nice home. But we also recognize that there are any number of people who have all those things but are still pretty miserable inside themselves. So we begin to look more deeply and see that it's not our *stuff* but our *actions* that make us happy or unhappy. Do the right thing and you feel good about yourself; do the wrong thing and your conscience will haunt you until the end of time.

The problem with this is that most of us have noticed that as often as not, good things happen to bad people, and bad things happen to good people. And although we may think that "doing the right thing" should be its own reward, life viewed from this level doesn't seem remotely fair.

It's thoughts like this that lead many people in a more internal direction in their pursuit of happiness and well-being, and we quickly see that, as we discussed in Session One, it's not what happens but what we *think* about what happens that determines our experience. So we begin experimenting with things like affirmations and positive thinking, sure that if we could just control the flow of thoughts through our own brains, we'd have the key to lifelong happiness.

A lot of people get stuck at this level of understanding because of one simple, innocent mistake—they attribute their inability to think only positive thoughts to a lack of skill or effort on their part instead of recognizing that the theory itself is based on an incorrect premise: the idea that you can actually control which thoughts come into your head.

When you really stop to think about it, you realize that you can only choose which thoughts to dwell on and make important, not which ones pop into your head at any given moment.

This is where people come to what seems like a real sticking point. As one of my clients once put it, "If happiness doesn't come from what I have or what I do, and I can't choose my thoughts, doesn't that leave me kind of screwed?"

That's certainly the conclusion some people come to. They decide that happiness is completely outside their control, and they give up on the pursuit. Often they actually begin to feel better when they stop trying so hard to be happy, leading them to another false conclusion: that happiness can only be pursued indirectly.

The reason why that's a false conclusion is because it still makes happiness into a "thing"—something we can have or not have, pursue directly or indirectly, successfully get, or, if we're not careful, lose.

Some people, in their pursuit of connection and well-being—or as we're calling it, "happiness"—decide that since they can't control which thoughts come into their heads, the thing to do is to try to stop thinking altogether. For reasons you'll understand in a few minutes, this seems to work, leading them into a complex set of routines, prayer, meditation practices, and a variety of other disciplines all designed to at least temporarily stop thought. Since feelings of peace and well-being often follow these practices, the practices themselves appear to be the means to a happy end. But the problem with all of them is that they take practice—and while that may seem a small price to pay for such a precious jewel, the vast majority of people are unwilling or unable to put in 20 years of daily meditation for 20 minutes of daily bliss.

So let's take another look at our fundamental premise:

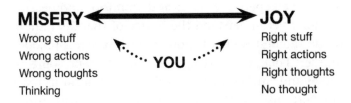

The one thing inherent in all these notions is the idea that misery and joy are somehow things that are outside us, and that we need to do things in order to get them. But here's another way of looking at things, one that stands our usual notions of where to go to find well-being on their head:

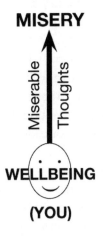

A quick look into a baby's eyes will reveal that we're born at peace—in tune with the infinite, in touch with our bliss, resting in the well of our being. But even when we're babies, our very human needs from time to time interfere with our connection to this innate well-being. We experience physical discomfort, and because we don't yet understand the source of that discomfort, we do the best we know how to do—we scream bloody murder! Then, to our delight and amazement, someone comes and "makes it better"—they feed our hunger, dry our bottoms, entertain our nascent brains with funny noises and roller-coaster-type movements . . . and before we know it, we're nestled back into the bosom of our innate well-being.

Over time, it's the most natural thing in the world for us to begin to connect and even attribute that return to well-being to the people or activities that seem to be causing it—we're okay because Mommy loves us; we're okay because Daddy protects us; we're okay because the people around us, for the most part, appear to have our well-being at heart. And then one day we do something in our joy that Mommy or Daddy doesn't like—we splash paint on a wall or cry when Daddy is tired—and suddenly the ocean of love we're used to swimming in is filled with sharks and other monsters too horrible to mention. Before long, we've bought into the myth that love and well-being exist outside us, and the need for a persona is born.

But well-being—happiness, connection, love, peace, spirit—is our essential nature. So all our attempts to capture these feelings from out in the world, no matter how well intended and practically followed, are doomed to fail. Not because happiness and well-being are unattainable, but simply because it's impossible to find what has never been lost.

This leads us to our second secret:

**Well-being is not the fruit of something you do;
it is the essence of who you are.
There is nothing you need to change, do,
be, or have in order to be happy.**

The reason why this understanding of the source of well-being is so significant is that so much of our energy and time is squandered in pursuing goals and projects and financial incentives and relationships that we believe will "make" us happy. And so much of the stress and strain we experience in our lives is brought on by our misguided attempt to make ourselves feel better by having, doing, or achieving the right things.

Simply put, what we attribute our good feelings to will determine what we do and where we go to get more of them:

- If I think my well-being comes from being around a particular person, I'll do all sorts of things I wouldn't otherwise do and put up with things I wouldn't otherwise put up with in order to keep that person around.

- If I think my well-being comes from my work or my income, then I'll overinvest in that job and even be willing to betray what I believe in to preserve or enhance it.

- If I think my well-being comes from a food or drug, I'll do whatever it takes to get hold of that food or drug the next time I'm feeling in need of another "hit" of good feelings.

Because of the principle of the self-fulfilling prophecy, whatever I believe will continue to appear to be true. The world is what we think it is, and when we tell ourselves that any of these things will make us happier, they will—at least for a time.

But when you begin to understand that well-being is your nature, not a goal to be pursued, you'll quickly realize that all you have to do to get it back is to turn your attention from the outside in.

Do You Really Need to Work on Your Self-Esteem?

Jeremy had joined a multilevel marketing company and hired me to help him boost his self-esteem. He'd heard a motivational speaker talking about the importance of self-image and self-worth in creating success and had decided that what was holding him back was his low opinion of himself.

In our first session together, I asked him how he knew that low self-esteem was what was holding him back. He looked shocked.

"Don't you need high self-esteem to succeed?"

Having worked with some of the most successful people in Hollywood, the majority of whom had the self-esteem of a gnat, I knew that most of what people call "self"-esteem is actually based on how things appear to be going in their lives, and goes up and down on a daily basis.

I then told Jeremy the story of when my son Oliver, age six, was first learning to play baseball. A few weeks into the season, he came to me and said, "Daddy, I want to quit—I don't want to play anymore." When I asked him why he wanted to quit, he shocked me by saying, "Because I'm crap at baseball."

Now, if I'd really thought that self-image and self-esteem were the keys to success, I would have given him the "Go get 'em, tiger" speech. I would have talked to him about how he needed to "believe to achieve" and "whether you think you can or you can't, you're right."

But when he said to me, "I'm crap at baseball," I said to him, "Yes, you are. But here's the question: do you want to get good at it?"

Well, his little eyes lit up. It had never occurred to him that being good at baseball was something you could learn, not something you were born able to do. I said to him, "Here's how we do it. Every day you're gonna throw me 50 throws and I'm going to throw you 50, and we're going to take 50 swings, and I guarantee within a month you're going to be pretty good at this."

And we did, and he was, and strangely enough, he started liking it a whole lot more as well.

The reason self-image is so important, or so the experts tell us, is that we'll inevitably live up or down to our self-image—that is, we'll become more and more like the person we think (or are afraid) we really are. So if someone believes or "sees themselves" as shy, they'll tend to behave shyly; if they see themselves as confident, they'll tend to behave in a more confident manner.

This leads to a host of Level I and Level II interventions. At Level I, we use our physiology to create a greater sense of confidence by standing up straight, putting our shoulders back, and looking people straight in the eye. We might back this up with both affirmations ("I am confident, I *am* confident, I am *confident!*") and affirmative actions of the "feel the fear and do it anyway" variety.

At Level II, we go to work on the self-image directly. We use hypnosis, relaxation, and guided visualization to change the pictures we have of ourselves in our mind. We run movies of our past successes and condition ourselves over 21 days or 30 days or however long it takes for us to begin to see ourselves in a new light.

Now, it's important to point out that this will have a powerful effect on the way we are in the world. But even if I'd done all that with Oliver, he would still have been crap at baseball—he just would have *thought* he was good at it.

This is echoed by a 2003 global study into the relationship between self-esteem and math ability in middle-school students. Of the ten countries with the highest level of student confidence, only Israel and the United States scored higher than average on the international test, and their scores were far below those of the much less confident students in Japan, Korea, Hong Kong, and Taiwan.

When I suggested to Jeremy that rather than work on his confidence, self-image, or even self-esteem, he should work on his business and the creative art of selling, he seemed a bit disappointed. But I then talked with him about the true source of self-esteem: his own innate well-being. I pointed out that when we take our focus off creating a more beautiful mask and put it toward uncovering our highest, deepest self, we discover that underneath the mask and underneath all the thoughts about what's wrong with us is something really rather wonderful.

In the end, Jeremy decided that he would rather spend his time being happy and going for what he wanted than going for what he wanted in the hopes that it would one day make him happy. In less than a year of connecting with the diamond of his essence, he had become a "diamond" in his network as well.

Here's a simple experiment that will allow you to experience this secret for yourself. . . .

Self-Improvement Vacation

1. Take a week off from working on yourself in any way. Don't try to change, improve, or fix yourself—just enjoy hanging out with your work, your hobbies, and your loved ones.

2. If you can't bring yourself to take the whole week off, take a few days off.

3. If you can't bring yourself to take a few days off, just take one.

4. If you can't even take one day off from putting nail polish on your diamond, repeat Step 1.

In a nutshell:

- Well-being is not the fruit of something you do; it is the essence of who you are.

- There is nothing you need to change, do, be, or have in order to be happy.

- You are a diamond, buried in horse crap, coated in nail polish.

- If you want to get better at something, work on your craft, not on yourself.

Don't worry if your life hasn't completely transformed just yet! The most common experience my clients share when we start working together is that nothing much seems to be happening until they turn around at some point and notice just how much *has* happened.

Remember, you can take as much or as little time as you want before you move on to the next session.

Have fun, learn heaps, and happy exploring. . . .

The Problem with Goals

"I dread success. To have succeeded is to have finished one's business on earth, like the male spider, who is killed by the female the moment he has succeeded in courtship. I like a state of continual becoming, with a goal in front and not behind."

— George Bernard Shaw

Why Does a Bird Sing?

A teacher who had received much acclaim for his insights and discourses into the nature of the universe was asked by one of his students what difference he hoped to make in the world through his teaching.

After a few moments' thought, the teacher replied that he had no such hopes.

"Those who can truly hear what I have to say don't really need me to say it; those who can't hear could listen until I was hoarse and could no longer speak without changing in the slightest."

The student was confused.

"But if you can't make a difference with your ideas, why do you teach at all?"

The teacher smiled.

"Why does a bird sing?"

How to Get What You Want

> *"The best way to predict the future is to create it."*
>
> — Peter Drucker

Let's begin our time together in this session by taking a quick look at the three main ways people have learned to go for and get what they want . . .

1. Acquisition

The school of acquisition has been the dominant one in Western culture for many years, and its teachings can be summed up in a sentence:

If you want it, go and get it!

From the ancient Mongol hordes to the modern titans of business and industry, our society tends to reward and hold up as heroes those men and women who have gone after what they wanted with enthusiasm and passion. (If they happened to trample a few people on the way to the top . . . well, it's unfortunate, of course, but those are just the casualties of war.)

In the acquisition model of the world, the stuff of life is out there somewhere, and your job is to go and get it. Acquisition-based thinkers often see life as a case of the "haves" versus the "have-nots," and shift between the roles of hero and victim in a "dog eat dog" world.

On the plus side, graduates of the school of acquisition have helped create ancient and modern empires and contributed to tremendous advances in science, medicine, and business; on the down side, they have also contributed to a world culture where the strong tend to look down on the weak and wonder why they don't just get off their lazy behinds, try harder, and "go and get it" for themselves.

2. Attraction

While the school of acquisition has been in full session for the past 2,500 years or so, the school of attraction has been quietly holding classes in hidden caves and New Thought churches, its teachings disseminated through secret texts, biblical parables, and New Age gurus.

The school of attraction teaches:

Like attracts like.

Thoughts become things.

and

You become what you think about.

These "secret" teachings and principles of attraction were often suppressed by the ruling elite, or so the story goes, because they placed the power within each individual, although the true source of that power is often attributed to God or a benevolent vibratory universe.

Many of the great men and women throughout history, from ancient religious icons to Renaissance men like Leonardo da Vinci and Sir Isaac Newton, are known to have studied the ancient texts of the school of attraction.

So now that this "secret" teaching is no longer a secret, why isn't everybody living the life of their dreams?

A woman who wanted to hire me as her coach told me that she had been deeply inspired by what she had been reading about the law of attraction. She had already applied these teachings to attract a new job, a great apartment, and a boyfriend who, in her words, "actually seems to really like me."

When I asked her what she hoped to get out of our work together, she was quiet for a few moments before somewhat shyly telling me, "I'm terrified that it will stop working, and I'll go back to being miserable and alone."

Here's the problem with the law of attraction:

People are attempting to use the principles of attraction as a new set of tools for acquisition.

Instead of actually shifting the basis of their approach to life to one of planting seeds of kindness, beauty, and love and reaping the harvest of a bountiful life, people are attempting to get a better parking space (or indeed a better car, boyfriend, or bank balance) by "thinking the right thoughts."

The source of the problem lies in the reason people want the car, boyfriend, or bank balance in the first place—because they believe having what they want will "make" them happy. But a closer look at the teachings of the school of attraction reveals that it works the other way around: *it is the energy of happiness that attracts the good things into our lives.*

Do the principles of attraction really work? In my experience, absolutely. But if you use them to try to manipulate the universe into giving you what you think you need to be happy, you're as likely to manifest frustration and self-doubt as that shiny new husband or loving automobile.

This leads us to a third way of thinking about getting what we want in our lives . . .

3. Creation

"People are always blaming circumstances for what they are. I don't believe in circumstances. The people who get on in this world are the people who get up and look for the circumstances they want, and, if they can't find them, make them."

— from *Mrs. Warren's Profession,*
by George Bernard Shaw

When I first ask people what they want, they generally go up into their heads to order off an invisible menu of possibilities that have been programmed and conditioned into their brains throughout their lives. For many of us, that menu is so limited that "Nothing seems to inspire me" is a common complaint. We don't know what we really want, so we go for the best thing we can find, assuming that something will be better than nothing but ultimately feeling uncreative, unsatisfied, and unfulfilled by what we get.

This is one of the reasons why even a traditional coach can be such a huge help in moving forward—

the coach generally has access to a larger menu with more choices available, consequently opening up new possibilities in the minds of his or her clients.

But while asking "What do you want?" with intention and awareness can certainly get at the real desires lurking underneath the straitjacket of societal acceptability, an even more powerful question is this:

What would you love to create?

When we come to the table as creators, we're no longer limited by whatever happens to be on the menu, because we know we can always go into the kitchen and cook up something wonderful of our own.

And what if, instead of seeing ourselves at a cosmic restaurant, we viewed our lives as a blank canvas; a musical score waiting to be written; or even a raw, unformed lump of clay? We would then be free to create absolutely anything—and if we don't like what we've created up until this point, we can always throw it away and start again.

Then the natural artistry you were born with as a child has the space to come out and play, and circumstances stop being "good" or "bad," or "right" or "wrong," but are simply the raw materials for your next creation.

The reality is, you're infinitely creative—and when you take the best of what's inside you and use it to create from, things like success, abundance, loving relationships, and a meaningful legacy stop being goals to be pursued and instead become the natural fruits of your creation. And therein we find the fundamental differences between these three models of success:

— **Acquisition-based thinking** places the power outside us in the visible physical world. If we want some of that power for ourselves, we need to go out and get it. When we don't get what we want, it's either because the world is rigged against people like us or we just aren't trying hard enough.

— **Attraction-based thinking** places the power outside us in the invisible metaphysical world. If we want to tap into that power, we need to align our thoughts, feelings, intentions, and desires. When we don't get what we want, it's either because God/the universe has a higher plan for us or we just aren't thinking positively enough.

— **Creation-based thinking** recognizes that the power is (and always has been) inside us. We access that power through the choices we make about how to be (our "ground of being"), how to see (our attitude, or "angle of approach"), and what to do (the words we speak and the actions we take). When we don't get what we want, it's either because we haven't yet found a way or it's just taking more time than we want it to. No blame, no fault, no shame. And when getting what you want stops being about you and becomes more simply about what you want, it also gets a whole lot easier.

A Great Big Game of Fetch

My two dogs, Mishka and Abby, have very different personalities. Mishka is bored unless engaged in her favorite game, which, as you might imagine for a dog, is "fetch." You take her bone and throw it as far as you can, and she chases it as fast as she can. Then she brings it back to you and asks (well, begs) you to throw it again. She wants to play fetch continually, and I've occasionally speculated that if I let her, she would keep chasing that bone right up to the point where she collapsed of physical exhaustion.

I call Mishka a "goal dog," because her behavior is similar to what I see in compulsive goal setters. They continually set goals in every area of their lives, driving themselves forward relentlessly toward the ever-receding goal of "making it." They rarely stop to consider what they would do if they did make it, and those who do succeed (at least by society's standards) often find themselves bored and empty until they throw themselves back into the fray.

Essentially, compulsive goal setting is like playing a game of fetch with yourself—you throw the bones as far as you can (set the biggest goals you can imagine), and then chase after them with hyper-focused attention and continual action. The problem comes when your happiness and self-worth are the bones.

For most compulsive goal setters, their sense of well-being comes from how well they think they're doing. And since they're constantly raising the bar on what "success" and "making it" mean, they're never doing well enough to feel happy and worthwhile. There's always more action to be taken and more targets to be reached, so there's never a sense of being content right where they are now. And, I occasionally speculate, if they let themselves, they'd keep chasing those goals right up to the point where they collapsed of physical exhaustion.

My other dog, Abby, is more of what I call a "river dog." I call her this based on the writing of supercoach

Earl Nightingale (founder of Nightingale-Conant), who described "river people" as being those who "are happiest and most alive when they're in the river—in whatever business or career or profession it happens to be. And success comes to such people as inevitably as a sunrise. In fact, they are successes the moment they find their great field of interest; the worldly trappings of success will always come in time."

Abby loves the park, and she loves the house. She loves going for a run with my son, but she seems equally happy and content to hang out on the sofa with our cats. In fact, wherever Abby is, she throws herself into the mix without ever seeming to need things to be a certain way.

Bizarrely, the one game Abby will almost never play is fetch. You can throw her bone as often as you like, but unless you go and get it yourself, it will never be seen again.

When it comes to us human beings, I think of these two approaches to life as being less about personality types than behavioral choices. In any given moment, we can decide that what we have isn't enough and look around for something to fill in the gaps, or we can decide that what we have is exactly what we want. We can turn our "bone of happiness" into a bone of contention and throw it off into some imaginary future, or we can enjoy gnawing on it right here, right now.

Here's the third secret:

There's nowhere for you to get to— you're just *here.*

This thought can be disturbing at first to people who feel that "the next big thing" is continually just around the corner. But if they sit with it, most feel their shoulders begin to relax as their experience of the present moment deepens.

Of course, just because there's nowhere to get to doesn't mean you'll no longer travel—just that you'll no longer do so in order to get somewhere that's better than right where you're sitting now. It doesn't mean that you can't upgrade your car, your job, your finances, or even your relationship. It just means that if you do, it will be because you want to, not because you think you have to or you should.

I had a client named John who adamantly refuted the idea that there was no inherent goal in life. Rather than get into an argument with him, I showed him a cartoon I'd photocopied from a magazine of a business executive in a suit running on a treadmill with a dollar bill attached to his forehead, just out of reach.

John didn't find it remotely funny, but I could tell that it triggered some sort of insight inside him. Before our next session, he sent me this quote attributed to the comedienne Lily Tomlin:

> *"The trouble with the rat race is that even*
> *if you win, you're still a rat."*

A Backward View of Moving Forward

> *"Man is only truly great when he acts from passion."*
> — from *Coningsby,* by Benjamin Disraeli

passion (n):
a: ardent affection : LOVE
b: a strong liking or desire for or devotion to some activity, object, or concept

When I was at drama school in London, a number of successful actors and actresses came to speak to us about what life was like "in the real world." It used to always bother me that so few of them seemed to have followed the rules of written goal setting I kept reading about in my ever-expanding collection of books on how to succeed.

One of the most profound memories I carry from that time was when award-winning actress Rosemary Harris (best known for either *Boys from Brazil* or being Spider-Man's aunt, depending on your generation) took the stage. When asked what sort of steps she'd taken to build her career—one that had spanned theater, film, television, and more decades than she probably cared to remember—she said, to our surprise, "I've never had a career—or rather, I've only ever had a career backwards."

When we asked her to explain, she told us that, rather like climbing a mountain, she only ever paid attention to what was in front of her, making her decisions according to what opportunities were available to her at that moment and what she felt she would most enjoy doing. It was only at times like this, when she stepped back to look at her life from the outside in, that she realized she was having what most people would call a "career."

Inspired by Ms. Harris, when I first introduce this idea to my clients, I often ask them to participate in the following thought experiment:

Give Up Your Career Today!

1. If you could just give up your career today, what would you want to do with your time over the next month? The next year? (Remember, it's okay if what you would want to do is in exactly the same area as your former career!)

2. If you weren't trying to get anywhere, what would you want to do with your time?

3. If you decided to make your working decisions based on your highest passions, values, and desires, what would you choose to work on next?

Rather than downshifting their careers or downsizing their lifestyles, I find that when people "give up" on getting anywhere and focus instead on living their passion, doing more of what they love and want to do, they wind up working more consistently and more passionately than they ever did when pursuing their so-called career.

Of course, if you have no idea what you're passionate about, that can be a pretty daunting thought. So grab a notebook and a piece of paper—you're going to make two lists.

Label the first "Things That Energize Me." Label the second "Things That Drain Me."

Over the course of today and the rest of the week, fill in the two lists to the best of your ability. See if you can come up with at least ten items on each one.

Example:

Things That Energize Me	Things That Drain Me
Hanging out with my wife	Doing my taxes
Loving my children	Large groups of people I don't know
Teaching	Trying to build a "career"
Reading books	Computer glitches
Developing ideas	People who don't do what they say they will

Before your list is even complete, look for opportunities to do more of the things on your "energizer" list and to eliminate, avoid, or reduce the amount of time spent on things on your "energy drain" list. This will cause an immediate increase in your day-to-day energy levels, and before you know it, you'll find yourself feeling more positive, enthusiastic, and hopeful!

But What If I Love Setting Goals?

> *"Give me a stock clerk with a goal and*
> *I'll give you a man who will make history.*
> *Give me a man with no goals and*
> *I'll give you a stock clerk."*
>
> — J. C. Penney

One of the most famous studies to support the value of goal setting as an essential part of success is the famous "Class of 1953 Study at Yale University," which followed the lives of a Yale graduating class over a 20-year period. At the end of that time, the 3 percent of graduates who had clear, written goals had outearned the other 97 percent of the class combined.

An impressive statistic—if it were actually true.

In researching an earlier project, I discovered that there was no record of the study ever having been done at Yale, Princeton, or any other Ivy League university. Tony Robbins reported he had first heard the story from Zig Ziglar; Zig Ziglar couldn't remember where he'd first heard it, but he thought it was from . . . wait for it . . . Tony Robbins!

Now that's not to say that either of these people is dishonest or that goals are "bad." But in a world where there's nowhere for you to get to, the trick to goal setting is to fully involve yourself in making things happen without investing your self-worth or emotional well-being into their achievement.

I first learned this distinction from supercoach George Pransky, and it helped me to understand this secret at a much deeper level. In order to share the distinction with you, I'd like you to imagine that there are two separate elements involved in creating anything you want in the outside world:

1. The first is *mental and physical involvement*—
    the extent to which you put your creative and
    physical energies into the creation of that
    outcome.

2. The second is *emotional investment*—the extent to which you put your happiness, self-worth, and well-being on the line in your pursuit of an outcome.

There are essentially four ways in which these elements can combine in relation to any goal, problem, or circumstance you can imagine in the world:

Low Investment/Low Involvement

Low investment/low involvement is when you don't particularly care (or even know) what happens, and you're doing pretty much nothing to influence the outcome in any way.

Someone who doesn't care about sports will be unaffected by the outcome of an athletic competition. Someone who has no interest in a relationship, job, or world situation not only won't care how those things are going, they will do little or nothing to attempt to influence how things go in the future.

On the plus side, low investment/low involvement is an extremely low-stress and relatively easy way to be; the downside is, you miss out on both the fun of creation and the potential impact you could be having on your life and the world.

High Investment/Low Involvement

One of the few fistfights I've ever found myself in came when I misguidedly suggested to a British soccer fan that his team's loss that day to their cross-town rivals didn't really merit the amount of moral outrage he was expressing at the pub that night. This is, in fact, the lot of all true fans—their moods rise and fall with their teams' fortunes, yet apart from cheering loudly and offering up the occasional fervent prayer, there's nothing they can do to affect the outcome.

This is the high investment/low involvement dilemma—you care too much and do too little. While in some situations this is necessitated by circumstance (that is, it's unlikely your favorite team will ever let you onto the field to kick the game-winning field goal), the lack of action is more often due to learned helplessness and emotional paralysis—it seems as though there's so much to be done that you wind up feeling overwhelmed and doing nothing.

High Investment/High Involvement

Graduates of motivational seminars, social crusaders and political activists, and high-flying entrepreneurs and careerists tend to pursue their goals from a high investment/high involvement point of view. They work long hours, take massive action, do whatever it takes, and then ride the emotional roller coaster up through the thrill of victory and down into the agony of defeat. One minute they're on top of the world; the next they're down in the pits of despair.

In fact, how well they're doing often comes down not so much to whether you happen to catch them in an up or a down as to how long they've been riding the coaster. For while this can be an effective approach in the short term, it often leads to the burnout/dropout mentality that stops so many people from actually reaching their goals and even generates an actual fear of setting goals.

"Oh no, I'm not putting myself through *that* again," the former eco-warrior or bankrupt businessperson will say. Yet lowering your involvement (doing less, dropping out, not playing anymore, etc.) won't ultimately resolve your desire for change. It will simply give you a bit of time to lick your wounds and recover your spirit before throwing yourself back into the arena in the only way you know how.

Low Investment/High Involvement

The two best ways I know to lower your level of emotional investment in an outcome are:

- Get as clear as you can about what is in your control and what isn't.

- Really see that you'll be okay regardless of what happens and how things turn out— that your ultimate happiness and well-being aren't at stake.

Years ago, I decided to see what would happen if I engaged in an act of "happy activism"—that is, I'd do anything I could think of to get our local council to put a pedestrian crossing in at the intersection near our house, but I'd completely let myself off the hook about how things turned out, which I recognized lay well outside my control. While the process wound up taking more than a year, to my surprise the entire project was low-stress, extremely enjoyable, and, as it happened, resulted in a pedestrian crossing.

This is the real payoff of a low investment/high involvement/effortless success approach—you get all the fun of being creatively engaged without any of the stress of being emotionally invested. It's completely sustainable because it's not dependent on continual emotional refueling to keep you going. And by letting go of trying to control the uncontrollable (that is, what other people will do and how things will ultimately turn out), you ironically increase your influence and the probability of getting what you want.

So, What Do You Want to Create?

> *"You want what you want, whether or not you think you can have it."*
>
> — Robert Fritz

Surprisingly often, the people I work with are out of touch with their wants and dreams. When this happens, the place to begin is with a simple exploration of all the obvious and not-so-obvious dreams and desires that fuel both our occasional discontent with where we are and our hopes and expectations of the future.

The following questions are adapted from the "Success Made Fun" one-year program (available at: **www.geniuscatalyst.com**), and they invite you to cast a wide net in exploring the future you most want to create for yourself and for the world.

They are based on the recognition that we all have a multitude of thoughts and desires fighting for recognition inside us and that the first step in choosing which ones you want to engage with is to get them out of your head and onto paper. They can encompass every area of your life, from your health to your wealth, your home to your office, and yourself to your spirit.

As you go through this exercise, I want you to start a list of *possible* goals for yourself. These don't have to be accomplishable in a year, or even within your lifetime. Don't consider whether they're realistic or specific or fit any of the other "goal rules" you've been taught.

I'll give you some simple ways to refine your choices later in this session. For now, just make a list of as many things as you can think of in each section, and then, when you're ready, move on to the next.

1. "Should" Goals

We all have things we think we "should" do in order to make the most of the opportunities we're being presented with . . .

- What goals "should" you pursue in the next year?

- What goals would make you "a better person" if you accomplished them?

2. Logical "Next Step" Goals

Often, the goals we pursue are simply natural progressions from the ones we've been pursuing in the past . . .

- What do you feel are the sensible, reasonable, responsible objectives for you to go after next?

- Since you did what you did in the past year, naturally you'll _____ in the coming year.

3. *Déjà Vu* Goals

What are the goals you swore you'd reach last year . . . and the year before that . . . and the year before that? Finish these sentence starters:

- "By now, you'd think I would have _____."
- "This year, I'm finally going to _____."
- "If I don't _____ this year, I'm never going to do it!"

4. Somebody Else's Goals

In this section, make a list of all the goals you carry around that were handed to you by someone else. This isn't to say you don't share others' aspirations for you. It's simply valuable to note the role that other people's intentions have in shaping our own.

Get started by filling in the blanks below:

- "My father/mother was already _____ when (s)he was my age."

- "My father/mother always wanted to _____."

- "Everyone has always expected me to _____."

- "My partner/spouse/friends really wish I would _____."

◆

In these next few categories, I'd like you to move away from the goals the mind tends to set and drop down into your heart. As you go through these categories, do your best to let go of all preconceived notions of what you could, couldn't, should, or shouldn't have and reflect quite simply on what you actually *want*, whether or not you think you can have it or create it.

5. "Deep" Wants

- What do you want more than anything else in the whole wide world?

- What do you daydream about, even if you've never admitted it out loud before?

- What would be even more wonderful than that?

6. "Fairy Godmother" Wants

If your fairy godmother showed up, wand at the ready, to grant you any wish you desired, what would you ask her to wave her magic wand for?

- What would you want if you could have absolutely anything drop into your lap out of the clear blue sky, without having to do anything at all to attain, keep, or maintain it?
- What else would you want?
- What else?

7. "Happy" Wants

Sometimes we don't let ourselves dream big because we fear how disappointed we'll be if we fail (again!) to make our dreams come true:

- What would you want if you knew you didn't have to be unhappy about *not* getting it?
- If your happiness wasn't dependent on getting what you wanted, what would you want?
- If you were *already* happy, what would you still want to do, be, learn, or have?

8. "Naughty" Wants

Were you ever told as a child that it was wrong to want things, or at least to want what *you* wanted?

- What would you want if you believed that having it wouldn't hurt anyone else, make you a bad person, or betray anyone you cared about?

- If you didn't think, "I shouldn't want that," what would you want?

- What would you want if nobody was watching?

- What would you want if nobody cared?

9. "If Only" Wants

Your life is what it is, but what if it wasn't? Would you want different things from the ones you want now?

- What wants of yours are followed immediately by:

    "but I can't _____."

    "but I could never _____."

    "but I don't have _____."

- If you removed the "but . . ." what would you want?

- What would you want if only things were different?

- What would you want if you knew that you really could handle having it?

10. "Wow!" Wants

What could happen in the next day/week/month/ year that would make you go "Wow!"?

- What would you love to have more of in your life?
- What would you love to do?
- Where would you love to go?
- What would you love to learn?
- What are your "big-grin goals"—goals that bring a big grin to your face when you think about them and will bring an even bigger grin to your face when you actually create them?

Take your time going through these questions. You can write them down and carry them with you throughout the week, jotting down additional answers as they occur to you. When you're ready, we'll take the next step to working out what you really want to create in and with your life.

From Desire to Project

"If you have built your castles in the air, your work need not be lost; that is where they should be. Now put the foundations under them."

— Henry David Thoreau

In the last section, I shared one of my favorite ways of coaxing your true heart's desires out of your spirit, into your head, and down onto a piece of paper. Now we'll continue the process by refining your list in a way that will make it easy for you to take a high involvement/low investment approach to their creation.

Here's all you need to do:

1. Go through the list of creative possibilities for your life that you generated earlier in this session.

2. For each item on your list, ask yourself a simple question:

> *"Regardless of whether or not I think I can actually have this, do I really want it?"*

- If your answer is an unquestionable "yes," circle or highlight it.

- If your answer is an unquestionable "no," cross it off or delete it.

- If your answer is *anything* other than a no-brainer "yes" or a no-brainer "no," leave it off for now. (I'll explain more about why that is in our next session.)

3. Gather all your "yes" goals on a new list. You're going to divide this list into two—a "fairy godmother" list and a project list.

— A **"fairy godmother" list** is made up of those things that you would love to be, do, or have in your life but you aren't really sure if you're up for creating them. However, if they fell into your lap; they came to you out of a clear blue sky; or your fairy godmother showed up, waved her magic wand, and "Hey, presto!" they were yours, you'd be all for them.

This is a powerful list to have because it keeps you in touch with your fondest dreams and warmest desires, even if the circumstances for their creation don't seem to be slanted in your favor right now. Not only will you find that energy of desire to be a useful guide, but you'll also notice that items on this list have a habit of showing up when you least expect them to.

— Your **project list** is made up of those things that you want to take responsibility for and make at least a part of your life about creating. Whether or not these projects actually come off as planned, you'll feel good about having invested the time and energy into making them happen. This list will give you a way of organizing your efforts so you can get maximum reward for every action taken.

4. For each item on your "yes" list, ask yourself these questions:

- "Do I want to make part of my life over the next year about actively creating this?"

- "Do I want to invest my time and energy into making this happen?"

- "If this didn't lead to the result I wanted, would I still be glad I took the time to work on it?"

71

If your answer is anything but an unquestionable "yes" to all three questions, put the item on your "fairy godmother" list; otherwise, it can go on your project list.

Goals and Projects

Many of my clients have goals related to reaching a certain level of success in their lives. But once they've set the bar for themselves, they immediately take the focus off what it is they're trying to achieve and put it onto what is within their control—the process and projects through which they're most likely to achieve it.

For a salesperson, that may involve making a certain number of calls or submitting a high enough volume of proposals; for a writer, it might be writing a specific number of pages or spending a certain amount of time in the act of writing.

One CEO I worked with decided that he wanted to create a more loving relationship with his wife. He was unclear about how he could turn that goal into a project until it occurred to him that she always commented on how loved she felt when he took the time to do something that made her life easier, particularly since she knew how busy his own life was. So he created a simple project for himself: to engage in one deliberate act of service to his wife every single day for a year. While he did miss a few days along the way, his relationship had transformed long before the year was up. Better still, his wife began to return the favor—and he hadn't even told her about the project!

Here are a few distinctions that will help you make the shift from goal to project for yourself:

- Goals are always reached in the future; projects are worked on in the present.

- Goals are things you work toward; projects are things you work on.

- With a goal, your focus is on the desired result; with a project, your focus is on the daily action.

- With a goal, you're a failure until the moment you succeed; with a project, you're successful until the moment you fail.

Goals	Projects
In the future	In the present
Working toward	Working on
Focus on result	Focus on action
Failure until successful	Successful until failure

An Obstacle Course to Success, Revisited

How simple can it be to get what you want in life?

I'm writing this in my office. Let's say I want to walk outside to enjoy the California sunshine. Unless my legs suddenly give way or someone leaps out from behind my sofa and tackles me (a somewhat creepy, if extremely unlikely, possibility), I'm going to do it. In fact, short of an act of God or other unpredictable event, there are only two things that could stop me:

The first is that I might not really want to go outside. It might just be a "neat idea" that I read about in a magazine or I might have been told was good for my health. In that instance, I might think that I *should* go outside, but this is extremely different from actually *wanting* to go.

Of course, the second thing that could stop me from walking out the door would be some sort of obstacle. But if I really wanted to go outside, that wouldn't really matter. I could use my creative genius to find a way over or around that obstacle. Because when you really want something, the question isn't "How will you get it?"; it's "What could possibly stop you?"

Action Days

Sometimes all the psychological insight in the world won't get you unstuck or move you forward as quickly as simply taking action. That's why when my clients seem overly caught up in theories of why they're stuck, we book an action day.

To create an action day for yourself, simply enlist the help of a buddy or coach. Every hour on the hour, phone in to let them know what actions you intend to take that hour. Then, no matter what else you might be up to, call back an hour later to let them know what you've done and what you've got planned for the next hour!

When I was a child, my favorite sport to watch on TV (and on very special occasions in the stadium) was football. I spent years playing in my backyard and the school playground, and then when I was 12, my parents finally let me sign up to play in a "real" league. I was so excited that I couldn't wait to get into pads and transform myself into a pint-size replica of my gridiron heroes. However, the first day of practice was more like a military boot camp than my fantasies of football glory. If you've never thrown on the pads of a football uniform, the one thing you may not realize is how heavy they are, particularly when you're 12. In full uniform, we spent the practice doing push-ups and sit-ups and running so many sprints that several of us threw up in the grass by the side of the field.

Finally, at the end of that first practice, they set up a mini-game to let us show them what we had. Unfortunately for me, what I had left at that point wasn't really worth having. On the very first play from scrimmage, our quarterback threw the ball downfield in my general direction, only to have it intercepted right in front of me by one of the largest 12-year-olds I'd ever seen. Caught between my exhaustion, fear, and desire to prove my manhood, I gave chase and was actually closing in on him when one of the other team's players threw himself to the ground in front of me in a last-ditch attempt to trip me up. At that moment, time stood still. I realized I had a choice: to carry on in the lung-burning, leg-aching pursuit of my prey or to let myself trip over this would-be blocker and finally get a rest.

In the years since that moment, I've found that this same kind of decision faces us nearly every day in the pursuit of our dreams. Things come up between us and our goals—something we don't yet know how to do, an unexpected bill, an overprotective gatekeeper, a child who doesn't sleep, or a spouse who somehow doesn't quite grasp the magnificence of our vision. What we do in those moments is ultimately what determines our destiny:

- If we treat whatever stands in our way as an *obstacle,* we can bring the full creative resources of our mind to bear on the situation and find ways to get over, around, or through it.

- If we choose to use it as an *excuse,* we allow ourselves to be tripped up or otherwise stopped by it.

While I would love to say I leaped over that kid and carried on to save a touchdown, the truth is that I let my foot catch on his shoulder pad and tumbled to the ground. I thought I'd feel relief, but what I actually felt was embarrassment and shame.

Now, of course, I know there's no embarrassment in a 12-year-old taking himself "out of the game" when he's exhausted and frightened. But I've also realized as an adult what a shame it is to allow an obstacle to become an excuse.

This is what I've learned:

**If you really want what you want,
there's always a way for you to create it.**

Obstacle or Excuse?

1. What do you want? Write down at least one big goal and at least one smaller one.

2. For each goal, answer the question: "What stops you?" As I wrote in *You Can Have What You Want*, it will always appear to be to do with one of nine things: *information, skill, belief, well-being, other people, motivation, time, money,* or *fear.*

3. Notice whether you've been treating that thing as an obstacle or an excuse. In other words, have you been actively brainstorming ways to handle it, or have you been telling yourself, "Oh well, maybe next time"?

4. If it's just an obstacle, get yourself into a higher state and brainstorm it again. Bring in friends, bring in a coach, bring in whatever and whoever you need to blast that obstacle to smithereens!

5. If it's an excuse, you have two choices:

a. Turn it into an obstacle and go back to Step 4. You do this by bringing your best self and your full creative resources to bear on how to get past it.

b. Give yourself a break and let go of the goal. When you don't really want to do something, one excuse is pretty much as good as another.

In a nutshell:

- Obsessing about goals is like playing a game of fetch with yourself, using your happiness and self-worth as the bone.

- There's nowhere for you to get to—you're just *here*.

- If you really want what you want, there's always a way for you to create it.

You might want to take a break before moving on to the next session. You can stretch your legs, go for a walk, or just take some time to reflect on what you've been learning.

When you're ready, I'll see you in the next session.

The Simple Way
to Make Decisions

*"You do not need to leave your room. Remain sitting
at your table and listen. Do not even listen, simply wait.
Do not even wait, be quite still and solitary. The world
will freely offer itself to you to be unmasked. It has no
choice. It will roll in ecstasy at your feet."*

— Franz Kafka

The Abbot and the Monk

Many thousands of years ago, or so the story goes, the word of God was transcribed into written form. Because there were no word processors, photocopiers, or even printing presses, monks would painstakingly copy each original text by hand. It could easily take a year to complete just one document.

A young monk who had abandoned the search for worldly pleasures wanted to see for himself the ancient texts and drink directly from the source of all wisdom. He volunteered to help copy them, but soon realized that he was in fact not copying ancient texts at all. He was copying copies made by other monks, who no doubt had also spent their lives copying copies of the word of God.

In his enthusiasm and curiosity, he asked the abbot if it would be possible to check the original texts, which were stored deep in the vaults of the monastery. After all, the monk reasoned, if any mistakes had been made in the copies, they were now being spread from generation to generation.

The old abbot declined his request. He told the young monk not to worry about such things, and the young monk dutifully obeyed.

Years passed and the young monk was no longer young. Although his enthusiasm for life had somewhat diminished over the years, his hard work and years of dutiful service led to his being chosen as the new abbot when the old one died. Now, instead of filling his days copying ancient wisdom by rote, he found himself with time for contemplation and reflection. Soon his old curiosity and thirst for truth returned, and he took it upon himself to go down into the vaults at the heart of the monastery.

He stayed down there for months, poring over the ancient texts by candlelight, pausing only to pray, to sleep, and to eat the meals that were left outside the door of the vaults every morning.

One day when the young monk assigned to care for him came by to gather up the empty dishes, he heard what sounded like distant crying. Although going down into the vaults was strictly forbidden, the young monk opened the door, lit a candle, and made his way into the sacred heart of the monastery. There he found his beloved new abbot sobbing uncontrollably.

"What's the matter, brother?" the young monk asked the abbot.

The weary abbot looked hopelessly up into the gentle eyes of the young monk. "We've made a terrible mistake," he said. "The original word was 'celebrate' . . ."

You Already Know What to Do

In theory, making decisions should be one of the easiest things in the world for us to do. After all, we either want to do something or we don't. On those rare occasions when we're not sure, it doesn't really matter. We can make whatever decision we want, or even flip a coin, knowing that we can change our minds afterward if what we thought we wanted turns out not to be all it was cracked up to be.

So why is decision making so difficult so much of the time?

Mostly because we get caught up in our thoughts that the decision *matters,* and that in some way we could or should know in advance how things will turn out.

But what if you couldn't make a mistake? What if whatever you decided always turned out to be the best thing, given the range of choices and information you had available to you at that moment?

The secret of effective decision making is simply this:

What you decide will never impact your life as much as how you handle the consequences of that decision.

In other words, marrying the wrong person is just a mistake; staying married to them for the next 25 years and being miserable about it is a bad decision.

Choosing one job over another might be a mistake; giving up on your career and spending the rest of your life pining over what might have been is a bad decision.

Getting tipsy and embarrassing yourself in front of that hottie from the office might be a mistake; letting it define you as a loser, a drunk, or someone not fit for human society would be a bad decision.

What makes for good decisions is what executive supercoach John LaValle calls "good brain juice"—the clarity in your mind that comes from having good feelings going on inside your body. When you're in a clear state, you generally either know what to do or know that it doesn't particularly matter. When you're caught up in a low mood (something we'll explore in depth in our next session), spending all your time imagining the possible negative consequences of making a decision, you'll tend to struggle.

What can make things easier is recognizing that no matter what you decide, you can almost always change your mind.

I had a client a few years back who was trying to decide between two high-level job offers from rival companies. After much internal and external debate, he accepted the job from the more traditional company, only to realize a few days later that his heart really wasn't in that decision. Because he was willing to make what he wanted more important than any sort of embarrassment or self-image issues that changing his mind might have engendered, he went back to the recruitment teams from both companies and admitted that he'd made a mistake. While the traditional company was reluctant to let him go, the other company snapped him up in seconds, and to this day he is thriving in his new environment.

Here's one of my favorite exercises for demonstrating to yourself that when you let go of trying so hard to get it right, you already know what to do:

Think of a decision you'd like to make. It can be as seemingly inconsequential as where you'll have lunch today or as important as which person you'll marry or which career path you'll take. You're going to make this decision in the next 60 seconds.

Now, take out a coin and decide which of your options corresponds to "heads" and which to "tails."

Ready?

In a moment, I'm going to ask you to flip the coin. If it lands heads, you're going to take option A, and if it lands tails, you're going to take option B. Before I do that, you have to promise to abide by the decision of the universe, as signified by the coin flip. . . .

(Just for fun, before we go any further, which way do you hope it lands, heads [option A] or tails [option B]?)

Okay, the moment of truth has arrived. Take a deep breath, flip the coin, and see which way your life has landed.

(Quick question for you: How do you feel about that? Relieved? Excited? Disappointed?)

Here's the secret: if you played along, you almost certainly experienced a physical, visceral response to the flip of the coin. The way you felt before the coin was flipped and the way you felt afterward are fantastic access points to your inner wisdom.

Remember, it doesn't matter which way the coin landed. The feeling you have while it's in the air and the feeling after it lands will tell you all you need to know.

Confabulation and "Satisficing"

> *"Perfection [as parents] is not within the grasp*
> *of ordinary human beings. . . . But it is quite*
> *possible to be a good enough parent."*

— from *A Good Enough Parent,* by Bruno Bettelheim

The dictionary definition of the word *confabulation* as a psychological term is as follows:

> "To fill in gaps in one's memory with fabrications that one believes to be facts."

In other words, to "confabulate" is to make up plausible-sounding reasons for our often completely irrational decisions and actions. If you've ever watched a stage hypnosis show, you've probably seen the volunteers explaining quite rationally to the hypnotist why they were dancing like Mick Jagger or kissing a broomstick. That is confabulation in action!

Here's the problem with confabulation: when we confabulate (make up) "very good reasons" why we behave in the ways that we do, we're setting ourselves up for a fall. This is because the decisions we make, actions we take, and moods we find ourselves in are often based on little more than an unconscious reaction triggered by an unnoticed stimulus.

In Jonathan Haidt's wonderful book *The Happiness Hypothesis,* he cites numerous studies that show the power of these hidden triggers. As he says:

> . . . exposure to words related to the elderly makes people walk more slowly; words related to professors make people smarter at the game of Trivial Pursuit; and words related to soccer hooligans make people dumber.

Yet when asked, people will explain away these changes with far more rational-sounding explanations, like "I'm walking more slowly because I'm tired today," or "I did so well at Trivial Pursuit because I drew easy cards."

The simple truth is, we're designed in such a way that our unconscious programming drives our behavior. When our "rational" thinking mind steps in, it's more often to justify our actions than it is to steer the ship. This is one of the primary principles behind most forms of social influence and persuasion, be it in advertising, sales, marketing, or even psychology. (Do you really believe that "a diamond is a girl's best friend"? If you do, do you think you were born believing that?)

When we're willing to simply trust ourselves and follow our instinct without confabulating a series of "really good reasons" for what we've decided, we have a gentle rule of thumb for making decisions with impunity:

The number of reasons you have to do something is inversely proportional to how much you actually want to do it.

Since our reasons can't be trusted, the only real basis for making a decision is this:

Do you want to?

If you want to, do; if you don't want to, don't.

Will this always lead to making the best possible decisions?

No. Nor is it designed to.

In 1957, Nobel Prize–winning political scientist Herbert A. Simon introduced the term *satisfice*—that is, to make a choice that is both satisfactory and sufficient to meet the needs of the situation without necessarily being the absolute best of all possible options. He contrasted "satisficing" as a decision-making strategy with "maximizing" (choosing the *biggest* option) and "optimizing" (choosing the *best* possible option).

To better understand the distinction between these three strategies, consider these two examples:

1. Selling a House

— **Maximizing:** My goal with this strategy is to get the highest possible price. If I'm maximizing, I'll probably set my price high, then play potential buyers off one another in order to get their bids up. The person with the highest bid will win.

— **Optimizing:** My goal with this strategy is to get the best possible deal. If I'm optimizing, I'll probably first make a list of critical factors (price, timing, ease of dealing with the buyer, and so on), weighting each factor for its relative importance. I'll then evaluate each offer against the various criteria, seeking the optimal combination of factors.

— **Satisficing:** My goal with this strategy is simply to get a good enough deal. If I'm satisficing, I'll probably set a price and time frame for the deal at which I'll be happy and accept the first offer that meets those criteria. Even if I get a "better" offer later, I'll most likely stick with the original buyer as long as that person continues to meet my needs.

2. Grocery Shopping

— **Maximizing:** My goal is simple—where can I get the most groceries for the least money? I may change where I shop from week to week based on who's offering specials on the items I most want to buy.

— **Optimizing:** My goal here is a bit more complex, as I might introduce factors other than price into the decision. Which stores have the healthiest or best-tasting food? Which are the most convenient for me to shop at? Of those stores, I'll make my decision about where to shop, seeking to get the best possible combination of health, taste, price, and convenience.

— **Satisficing:** Once again, my goal is simple—a "good enough" place to shop. If I'm satisficing, I'll get my groceries each week at the most convenient store I can afford to shop in.

Although there may be situations in life where investing the extra time in maximizing or optimizing would be worthwhile, the vast majority of decisions we make each day can benefit from the "satisficing" approach.

Satisficing

Deliberately satisfice (that is, settle for "good enough") at least three times this week as a way of reducing stress and simplifying your life.

Notice how easy or difficult you find it to let go of the "quest for the best."

Wants, Whims, Fantasies, and Shoulds

The problem most people have when they first switch over to the simplicity of "Do I want to?" as a primary decision-making tool is in discerning between four kinds of apparent desires, which I call *wants, whims, fantasies,* and *shoulds.* Let's take a closer look at each of these in reverse order:

1. Shoulds

". . . musterbation is evil and pernicious. . . . If you didn't musterbate, then you wouldn't awfulize, terribilize, catastrophize, say 'I can't stand it,' and put yourself down. If you only stuck with, 'I'd like very much to do well, but I never have to,' you wouldn't then disturb yourself."

— Albert Ellis

Based on my very unofficial research over the past 20 years of working with people, the number one question people attempt to use to navigate their way through life is this:

What would be the right/best/smartest thing to do in this situation?

The problem with this approach is that (a) there's no way of knowing the "right" answer until afterward, and (b) most of us hate being told what to do, even if we're the ones doing the telling.

Here are some key words and phrases that will let you know that your apparent "desire" is more likely a "should":

- "I should/shouldn't . . ."
- "I must/mustn't . . ."
- "I have to/ought to/need to . . ."
- "People are supposed to . . ."
- "Of course . . ."
- "Because . . ."
- "It makes sense to . . ."

2. Fantasies

"This is my ultimate fantasy: watching QVC with a credit card while making love and eating at the same time."

— Yasmine Bleeth

Fantasies are those things that sound fantastic but that in reality you'd be extremely unlikely to enjoy. For example, most married men and women have at some point fantasized about having sex with someone other than their partner. And if all you did was focus on the bit of the fantasy that took place in the bedroom (or boardroom or kitchen table or . . . well, you get the idea!), that would seem like a pretty great idea. But run the movie forward a bit. See yourself having to go home to your spouse and explain where you've been. See yourself getting into arguments about why you want to work late (again) or need to go on that extra business trip on the weekend of your anniversary. See yourself getting into arguments with your "secret" lover about why you can't keep pretending to work late, go away for the weekend, or leave your partner. If you have children, watch them getting caught up in the mistrust, anger, betrayal, and possible dissolution of your marriage. And now ask yourself if that's what you really want. . . . (I'll wait.)

Fantasies are generally enjoyable and perform an important function—they relieve stress, boredom, or whatever other way your unhappiness is currently manifesting itself. But for the most part, acting on a fantasy is a waste of time and energy. As we discussed in our second session together, changing the world is the worst possible way to change how you feel.

To test whether your desire is authentic or just a pleasant fantasy, take at least three tangible action steps toward making it real. If you can't, won't, or feel horrible once you do, you'll know it's probably worth letting it go!

3. Whims

"My wife tricked me into marrying her.
She told me that she liked me."

— McLean Stevenson

A whim is a momentary want, generally triggered by some external stimulus or internal mood. While whims can be useful clues as to what kinds of things you would enjoy doing, being, and having, their motive energy is fragile and difficult to sustain.

Here are three useful rules of thumb when it comes to following a whim:

1. If your "whim" is seemingly positive, life enhancing, and easy to follow, act on it as soon as possible. If you wait even one day, the spark of energy it brought with it will likely be diminished.

2. If your whim would require a major investment of time and energy, wait at least 72 hours (ideally a week) before doing anything about it. If the impetus to act is still there, take it!

3. If your whim is in any way negative, destructive, or threatening to yourself or others, leave it alone. Internal guidance is a lot kinder than you think; and even if a major life change is called for, there's invariably a gentler, kinder way of enacting it.

4. Wants

". . . why do they always teach us that it's easy and evil to do what we want and that we need discipline to restrain ourselves? It's the hardest thing in the world—to do what we want. And it takes the greatest kind of courage."

— from *The Fountainhead,* by Ayn Rand

Why does wanting get such a bad name in spiritual circles?

Perhaps it's because of its origin as a word that indicated a lack, as in the children's rhyme:

For want of a nail the shoe was lost,
For want of a shoe the horse was lost,
For want of a horse the rider was lost,
For want of a rider the battle was lost,
For want of a battle the kingdom was lost,
And all for the want of a horseshoe nail.

Perhaps it's to do with the Buddha's notion that desire is the root of all suffering. But the desire that the Buddha was referring to was replete with attachments and aversions—a sense that you "need" something to happen or your life just won't be worth living. That isn't wanting at all—it's craving. It's believing that your happiness is dependent on actually *getting* what you want.

The kind of wanting I'm referring to here comes from the heart and from the spirit. It's simple, it's clean, and it's pure. It's not a craving, and it's not a need. It's just a want—something that you're drawn toward and would welcome into your life. This is the kind of desire that if you learn to listen to it, follow it, and even surrender to it will guide you to a life more wonderful than you can ever imagine.

While this simple (but by no means easy) formula has led my clients, students, and me into ever-higher realms of both inner and outer success, I've also noticed that those people who resist following their own joyful guidance as a way of being in the world have many variations of one basic concern:

> *"If I just did what I wanted all day long,*
> *I'd never get anything 'important' done."*

Navigating by Desire

This week, before deciding on any course of action, ask yourself, "Do I want to?"

Wherever possible, allow your answer to influence your decision and guide your choice.

Do this irrespective of whether or not you're "in the mood." If you do, you'll notice that your mood will begin to change "all by itself."

Although I know from experience that this isn't true in practice, I can see that in theory it seems as though it should be true. After all, not many people wake up in the morning thinking, "You know what I'd love to do today? I'd love to do the laundry and feed the kids before taking the car in to the garage on my way to a job I'm only doing because it pays the bills! Whoo-hoo!"

But what often resolves this apparent conflict for my clients is when I explain the difference between navigating by desire and navigating by mood:

- Navigating by *desire* means you base your decisions about what to do or not do on the question "Do I want to?" If the answer is "yes," you do your best to move forward; if the answer is "no," you do your best to stay put.

- Navigating by *mood,* on the other hand, is when you attempt to base your decisions on the answer to the question "Do I feel like it?" If you don't feel like doing something, you put it off until later; if you do feel like it, you move forward.

While at first these two ways of making decisions seem similar, they take people in two completely different directions. Since our moods are often tied up in old habits and patterns of thinking (more on this in Session Five), following them tends to just create more of the "same old, same old" in our lives. Somehow, we just don't get around to making those changes we know we'd love to make and things that seem as though they'll take too much effort are put off until the last minute or aren't done at all.

Wanting, however, is a living, breathing, fluid process. Each time you do what you want (or don't do what you don't want), your actions seem effortless, and inspired ideas become almost commonplace. Over time, it becomes easier and easier to read and follow your inner compass. Life gets a lot simpler, and the pursuit of success becomes a lot more fun.

The Wisdom of Common Sense

There is a very old joke about a man who goes to a doctor.

"Doctor," the man says, attempting to lift his arm over his head, "it hurts when I do this."

The doctor looks at him sagely and says, "Don't do it!"

This kind of common sense/innate wisdom approach to life is nearly always available to us, but we spend so much of our time caught up in the whirlwind of our thoughts that we don't notice it. And even when we do notice it, we'll often ignore it, hoping that our intellect can find a different answer more in keeping with what we hope will turn out to be true.

I was explaining this idea in a meeting with a potential corporate client one day when one of the women in the room asked for an example. I went with the first one that popped into my head—that nearly every woman I've talked to who has come out the other side of a bad marriage has told me that she knew not to marry the guy at some point before getting far enough down the aisle to say "I do."

What Do You Want to Be Doing Right Now?

Anytime you're not quite sure if you're doing what you really want to be doing, try this little experiment in turning up the volume on your inner guidance:

Put the words "I want to . . ." in front of a description of whatever it is you're actually doing.
For example:

- "I want to be writing this chapter."
- "I want to be sipping tea."
- "I want to be worrying about money."

If it becomes apparent that anything on your list isn't actually what you want to be doing, *stop doing it!*

Before I could even finish my example, another of the women in the room burst into tears. It turned out that she was engaged to be married and was doing her best to ignore her wisdom because she didn't want to "let anyone down."

"Besides," she asked me, "how do I know whether or not that's some kind of inner wisdom or just fear?"

I was tempted to say, "Ask your wisdom," but I offered her the following guidelines . . .

- Wisdom is ever present and always kind.

- Wisdom is sometimes soft but always clear.

- Wisdom comes most often in the midst of inner quiet.

- Wisdom feels right, even if it doesn't always feel good.

- Wisdom often comes disguised as "common sense," but in reality is extremely uncommon in usage.

Your wisdom is right there inside you, just waiting for you to allow it to guide you. You need only be quiet and listen—when you relax into it, you'll almost always know what to do.

What Do You Know?

1. Choose an area of your life that you would like to have some additional insight into—for example, health and diet.

2. Putting that topic aside for a moment, begin to write or recite aloud a list of things you "just know." Start with the screamingly obvious, for example:

- "I know that today is _____."
- "I know my name is _____."
- "I know that I went to school at _____."
- "I know I am _____ years old."

3. After about a minute, or whenever you feel that you're "in the flowing of your knowing," begin to make pronouncements about whatever area you've chosen to explore. Don't worry whether what you're saying is "true" or "right"; just keep talking for at least another minute and notice what you notice. For example:

- "I know that eating carrots gives me indigestion."
- "I know that having a potato at bedtime helps me sleep better."
- "I know that I can take better care of my teeth and gums."
- "I know that central heating dehydrates me."

Make note of any of your "knowings" that have the ring of truth about them. If you're moved to do so, follow up on your insights with appropriate action.

> **In a nutshell:**
>
> - You already know what to do.
>
> - What you decide will never impact your life as much as how you handle the consequences of that decision.
>
> - The number of reasons you have for doing something is inversely proportional to how much you want to do it.
>
> - Do you want to?

I'll leave it to you to decide whether to move on to the next session right away or take a break to let what you've been learning soak in. Of course, it doesn't really matter what you decide—after all, you can always change your mind later. . . .

Have fun, learn heaps, and I'll be waiting for you in the next session!

SESSION FIVE

Rainy Days and Mondays

*". . . life does not consist mainly—or even largely—
of facts and happenings. It consists mainly of the storm
of thoughts that is forever blowing through one's head."*

— Mark Twain

The Stonecutter and the Angel

Once upon a time there was a young stonecutter who looked with envy upon the rich merchant who employed him. One day he was muttering to himself about what it would be like to have such freedom and power when, to his amazement, an angel appeared and spoke the words "You are what you have said." In an instant, the stonecutter had become the merchant.

He was very happy with his lot until he saw the king of the land ride by with his coterie. "Now that's the way to live," he thought. Almost before he had asked, the angel had granted his wish and the merchant had become the king.

All was well until one beautiful summer's day when the king began sweating in his heavy royal garb. "What freedom and power the sun has," he thought. "It can float through the sky and call forth water from a king. That is what I would truly like to be."

As the thought appeared in his mind, the angel appeared to grant it.

Now the king had become the sun, and he reveled in his freedom and power as he floated high above the earth. But after a time, a cloud appeared and blocked the land from his view. When he watched the lightning burst forth from the cloud and heard the roar of the thunder, he knew that he was witnessing true freedom and power. Before he even realized what was happening, the angel had transformed him into a cloud.

What fun it was to pour rain forth upon the land! Wherever the man-cloud went, forests were washed away, and puddles became oceans in his wake. But no matter how hard he tried, there was one huge mountain made of stone that stood immovable and unaffected by his rain.

"Surely that is the ultimate power," he thought. "To stand tall in the face of any circumstance—that is true freedom and power."

In an instant, the angel had made it so, and the man could feel the incredible power of being an immovable object in the midst of any storm. Yet even as he was delighting in his immense strength and resilience, he could see a small man chipping away at his base with a pick and a chisel and a hammer.

"That man is even more powerful than I," he thought. "See how he is able to take stone away from me with just a few blows of his mighty tools. That is the kind of freedom and power I have always longed for."

The angel appeared and once again spoke the words "You are what you have said."

And with those words, the older but wiser stonecutter continued on his journey.

◆

A Simple Model of Emotions

Imagine this scenario:

You've had a really terrible day. You're tired and hungry and are torn between thinking about a problem that came up just before you left the office and the argument you know is looming with your partner about what happened last night.

Suddenly, a small child comes up to you and just looks at you.

How do you respond? What do you do?

Now shake that thought right out of your head and imagine this:

You've had a really wonderful day. Work went well, and you're on the verge of a breakthrough with one of your most important clients. Soon you'll be meeting up with the love of your life for a romantic candlelit dinner and more.

Suddenly, a small child comes up to you and just looks at you.

How do you respond? What do you do?

While most people have completely different reactions to the child in each scenario, what really fascinates me is how nearly everyone who participates in this "thought experiment" is able to think themselves into a higher or lower mood in a matter of seconds.

The reason for this is because you're using the same skills an actor uses to create emotion and every one of us uses to create our emotional experience of life: the power of imagination and thought.

Here's our fifth secret, the secret of emotional well-being:

Every emotion you experience is a direct response to a thought, not to the world around you.

The more clearly you see that your emotions are always reactions to your thoughts, not to the world, the easier it is to simply feel them and let them go. And the gift of that insight is that you stop needing to change the world in order to change the way you feel.

There's No Such Thing as a "Bad Day"

> *"We should be graceful with our low*
> *moods and grateful for our high ones."*
>
> — Richard Carlson

In Beth Henley's award-winning comedy *Crimes of the Heart,* three women reunite at their old family home to deal with the troubles in their lives, ranging from their mother's suicide to the youngest daughter's attempted murder of her wealthy fiancé. In the end, they draw the conclusion that both the suicide and the attempted murder stemmed from the women in question having "a really, really bad day."

When all their stories have been shared and a new level of understanding has been reached, the middle daughter comes to a remarkably unremarkable solution to all their problems: "We've just got to learn to get through these really bad days."

At our best, we all handle life remarkably well. We know what to do and tend to do it when it needs to be done. We follow our common sense and our wisdom and just naturally make the best decisions we can based on the information we have. But unfortunately, we don't always live life at our best. In fact, for many people the times spent in the comfort and care of their own wisdom and well-being seem far too few and far between.

What begins to give you control of this process, turning you from an apparent victim of circumstances back into the creator that you truly are?

Here's a corollary to the secret of emotional well-being:

**Your day doesn't create your mood;
your mood creates your day.**

When your mood is low, the world looks bleak; when your mood is high, you feel as if you can take over the world.

When your mood is high, your partner is the most wonderful person in the world; when your mood is low, they're a complete bastard.

The difference is, as always, not in the world, but inside you. And a deeper understanding of how it's being created will give you a whole lot more options about what to do about it.

Why Not Just "Think Positive"?

> *"The quality of the emotion equals*
> *the quality of the thought."*
>
> — Roger Mills

Since your emotions are a direct response to your thoughts, logic suggests that the only thing that will change them is to change your thoughts. So why not just think positive all day long, carefully weeding out all the negative thoughts until your garden of positivity is lush and you can live happily ever after?

Well, first off, have you ever actually tried that?

There is a famous episode of the television program *I Love Lucy* where Lucy Ricardo gets a job working on the production line at a chocolate factory. She's supposed to wrap each chocolate as it passes by, but once one gets by her and she tries to catch up, all the other chocolates start to pile up until she and the factory are a big gooey mess.

That's what usually happens when we try too hard to monitor the activity inside our heads. It all goes swimmingly until one thought gets by and then everything goes to hell.

This is why I've always liked the expression "train of thought," because it so accurately describes the way each thought that passes through our head invites us to travel with it. One thought of a childhood friend can lead you on a pleasant journey all the way back down through your youth; one thought about an argument with a loved one can carry you into paroxysms of rage or daydreams of escaping into the arms of another.

Yet our thoughts are simply internal conversations and mental movies that have no power to impact our lives until we charge them up by deciding they're important and real. And if we "empower" the wrong thoughts, making our negative fantasies seem more realistic than our external reality, it's like boarding a train to a destination we have no desire to actually reach.

That's why the important thing to realize about your thinking, particularly your "unhappy" thinking, is this:

It's almost never the 1st thought that hurts—
it's the 5th, or 50th, or even 500th that inevitably
comes when you follow a negative train of thought on
its rambling journey to destinations unknown.

This raises an important question: if you're never quite sure where a train of thought will lead you, how do you know which thoughts to engage with and which to let go?

The answer lies not in our thoughts but in our feelings. When you're feeling good (not "high" but happy, loving, comfortable, easy, well, etc.), that means your thinking is healthy and will probably take you in positive directions. When you're feeling bad (angry, frustrated, stressed-out, uncomfortable, unwell, and so on), chances are that your thinking is unproductive and whichever thought you might engage with will lead you somewhere you don't really want to go.

This gives us a remarkably reliable way of navigating through to our own wisdom. You can actually use your feelings as a sort of early warning system, like a traffic signal for trains of thought:

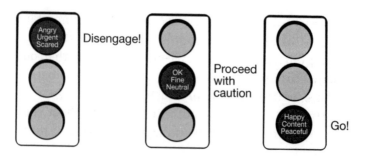

- If you're feeling bad, that's like a red light warning you to disengage from whatever toxic thoughts are in your mind. You don't have to try to stop thinking altogether; just don't climb on the train and don't fall for the sense of importance and sudden urgency your thoughts may seem to have.

- If you're feeling somewhat neutral, that's like a yellow light that says "Proceed with caution." It's possible that the thoughts racing through your mind are worth paying attention to, but if you feel your mood begin to drop, jump off whatever train of thought you've been traveling on and wait until your mood rises before you reengage with your thinking.

- If you're feeling content and at peace, you'll tend to think higher-quality thoughts—and those thoughts can lead you to some pretty wonderful places.

Of course, one of the problems with being in a low mood is that your point of view is often so distorted that you don't *realize* you're in a low mood!

Here are some pretty reliable indicators:

- You feel bad.
- Your sense of humor has gone missing.
- You have an all-or-nothing mentality, coupled with a sense of either urgency or *ennui*. You either feel that you *must* put an end to all your problems *now* or you feel that there's no point in doing anything about anything. Neither point of view is correct or particularly useful.

What's interesting to note is that the feeling of urgency is one of the most reliable indicators that what you actually need to do is slow down and take a break. Rather than try to "change your state" when you're feeling low, do your best to center yourself in the present moment, recognizing that no matter how urgent or pressing a course of action may seem, chances are it's just a thought.

In *You Can Have What You Want,* I share the story of how as a teenager I finally learned to recognize the difference between the suicidal trains of thought that had occupied my thinking for years and any actual desire to end my life. Once I recognized the "suicide thought" as just a thought, no more significant than any other, I was able to quickly let it go each time it arose. By not getting "on the train," my sense of fear and suffering diminished overnight.

In the same way, if you choose not to act on your thinking when you're feeling low, you'll find that as your mood lifts, the quality of your thinking will lift with it—and when you climb aboard a quality train of thought, it can take you a long way toward living the life of your dreams.

This is sometimes easiest to recognize in the case of small children. For example, my daughter Maisy came into our bed one night, sobbing that she'd dreamed that our cat had died and we'd had to bury her. No amount of reassurance (including the presence of the actual cat) would calm her until my wife agreed to remove the dream from Maisy's head. (For those of you not familiar with this process, we've found that it is most effectively done through the ear after a bit of struggle and accompanying sound effects!)

When I checked in to see how Maisy was doing the next morning, she told me that although the dream had indeed been successfully removed, she was still able to imagine the cat dying, which made her very, very sad.

And herein lies the point:

*It's not the thoughts that pass through
your head that impact your life;
it's the ones you take ownership of
and think about all day long.*

Thoughtspotting

During the day, if you notice yourself feeling down or a bit worried or unsettled, see if you can spot the thought behind the feeling. As soon as you've spotted it, let it go. You can imagine it as a stick that's become stuck in a river, and simply give it a nudge to set it free.

Here's an example of the typical thoughts that might pass through someone's head in any given minute on the way to work in the morning:

I'm going to be late, I just know I'm going to be late, I shouldn't have eaten that extra piece of cake last night, I'm such a fat disgusting slob, no wonder no one will ever find me attractive, boy, he is gorgeous, I wonder what it would be like to be with someone like that, I bet it would be wonderful, I have so much love inside me—it feels really good, but no one will ever know because I'm all alone, what was the name of that song I heard on the radio last night, oh no, I'm going to be late. . . .

Now, in and of themselves those thoughts are not a problem. You might experience a slight boost in your feelings when the happier thoughts float by and a slight dip in your mood when the more negative ones pass through, but if you let each thought pass without thinking about it too much, the thought stream will simply flow on quietly in the background throughout your day. But when you step in and start to actively think about thoughts, they can become a problem. For example:

I'm going to be late, I just know I'm going to be late, I shouldn't have eaten that extra piece of cake last night, I'm a fat disgusting slob, no wonder no one will ever find me attractive—why is this always the way? If only I had more willpower, I'm definitely going on that diet tomorrow, but what's the point, I never stick to anything, I'm such a loser . . . I need more cake!

It's easy to imagine where this train of thought might lead and the associated bad feelings and potentially poor decisions that could follow from it. The Toltec shaman don Miguel Ruiz describes this phenomenon as being "hooked" by a thought—and once we agree to give our attention to any given thought, it becomes more and more real to us over time and has more and more power over our lives.

The trick (if you want a less stressful, more enjoyable life) is not to call in the thought police, but rather to allow any and all thoughts to pass through your head unhindered. If you let a negative thought pass through your head without giving it a second thought (or a third, or fourth, or even fiftieth), it will have no impact on your life. But if you get hooked by it, dwell on it, make it important, and start to think about it and claim it for your own, then you'll become subject to its inevitable effects.

Here's a simple exercise about thoughts that can lead to some profound insights:

Thoughts Without a Thinker

1. Take a few minutes to really listen to your internal dialogue. You may find it easier to do this if you write it down in "real time," taking dictation, as it were, from that voice inside your head.

2. Notice the somewhat random nature of these thoughts. (If they seem very linear and organized, that's because you have been *thinking* them instead of simply *noticing* them.)

---

3. As best you can, allow each thought to pass through your mind without clinging to it or taking it over for yourself. If you do notice you've gotten caught up in a particular train of thought, just let it go or ride it out to its inevitable conclusion. Notice if a higher thought comes to take its place!

The Scale of Emotions

"Underneath every desire is the desire to feel good."

— from The Teachings of Abraham®

You'll find that as you step off a self-defeating train of thought, you nearly always move up one or two notes on the scale of emotions. While there are many of these "scales" floating around, the one I tend to use comes from supercoach Lester Levenson, the inspiration behind both the Sedona Method and the Release Technique, two excellent systems I often recommend that my clients learn and master.

Essentially, there are nine emotional states you can experience in relation to any goal or project you may be working on, depending on what's going on with your thinking. The higher up the scale you go, the better you'll feel, the more clearly you'll think, the more energy you'll have, and the more quickly and easily you'll be able to create what you want.

The Scale of Emotions

Peace
Acceptance
Courageousness
Pride
Anger
Lust
Fear
Grief
Apathy

Here are the nine "notes" of the emotional scale:

1. Apathy. Apathy is the "dead" feeling that so many people experience as a sort of depression or indifference to life. In relation to your goals, it stems from a kind of learned hopelessness: "Nothing you do is going to matter anyway," apathy tells you, "so you may as well not do anything at all."

Apathy is sometimes mistaken for peace because of the absence of emotional variance—the difference is, peace actually feels good!

2. Grief. If you feel a great sense of sadness or loss when you think about your goals, you're resonating with the frequency of grief. This is an evolution from the hopelessness of apathy to the helplessness of despair. "What you want *could* have happened," grief says, "but it won't—at least not for you, not anymore."

3. Fear. When you begin to see that it really is possible to have what you want, grief often gives way to fear. "You could have what you want," says fear, "but it would cost you so much that you'd regret it for the rest of your life—which might be over sooner than you think if you actually go for this!"

The important thing to remember is that if you're feeling fear, you've already turned a corner—you have moved from hopelessness to helplessness to possibility (albeit a vague and frightening one).

4. Lust. As you get more comfortable with the idea of having what you want, lust (as in need and greed) tends to kick in. This is for me the real meaning of the biblical phrase "the love of money is the root of all evil"—substitute "lust" for "love" and you can see how lusting after lucre could lead to all sorts of moral, ethical, and actual dilemmas. Lust says: "You can have what you want—and then you can get more, and more and more and more and more, and then everyone will do your bidding and you can take over the world!"

On the plus side, in order to lust for something, you have to have really begun to believe in the possibility of getting it.

5. Anger. The energy of anger burns hot. "Sure you can have what you want," anger rages, "but look at all these jerks who are trying to stand in your way. You deserve it—how dare they!"

There is actually a lot of energy in anger—it's just usually directed at your obstacles, not your goals.

6. Pride. Pride can be a tricky one, because to many people it feels really good. "Look at me," pride declares.

"Aren't I amazing to have already done so well and gotten so much of what I want?"

The truth is, you *are* amazing—but if your energy gets stuck in pride, it stops moving toward your goals and quickly slides back down into anger that you don't have more, lust to get it, fear of losing what you've already got, and grief anytime you actually lose what you thought was yours to keep.

7. Courageousness. Courageousness is the first truly "attractive" emotion in that it accepts the possibility that things might not work out but drives you on anyway. "Screw it!" courageousness declares. "Let's do it!"

8. Acceptance. There's an easiness to acceptance that says: "I have the serenity to accept the things I cannot change, the strength to change the things I can, and the wisdom to know the difference."

With acceptance, you're still moving toward your goals, but it's with a sense of ease and lightness that knows the journey is every bit as much of a prize as the destination.

9. Peace. In *A Course in Miracles,* readers are encouraged to make peace their only goal. This is because when you have peace in your mind and heart, you need nothing and have everything. Peace doesn't say much of anything, except to occasionally whisper, "Rest easy—all is well."

When we're at peace, we already have everything we need—and nothing is quite as creative as a need-less human being.

In order to move up the scale of emotions in relation to a project or goal, all you need to do is let go of your current thinking about that goal—in particular, the story that having what you want will in any way change your life for the better or for the worse.

As we talked about in Session Three, when you recognize that there's nowhere for you to get to and you don't really need what you want, you're free to have it—and that freedom is perhaps the ultimate goal.

Unconditional Happiness

One of the most comforting things for me is knowing that regardless of what's going on in my thoughts and my life, a deeper feeling is always available to me. Gratitude, compassion, and love are examples of these deeper feelings—deeper because they don't necessarily go up or down depending on what's happening around you.

When your mood is low (or even when it's not), you can reconnect to your higher wisdom by simply tuning in to the deepest, most wonderfully unconditional feeling you can find and hanging out in it as best you can.

Here's one last exercise you can do in letting go of thoughts and moving up the scale of emotions:

Creating above the Line

1. Write down three things you want in your life—one personal, one relational, and one financial. For example:

- "I want to be a size _____."
- "I want to get along better with my partner/kids."
- "I want to double my income next year."

2. Now, rewrite these wants in terms of "creating"— that is, "I am creating . . ." or "I am creating myself as . . ." If the rest of the want changes as a result, that's okay, too. Notice where you are on the scale of emotions when you think about your new goal statement. For example:

- "I am creating myself as a size _____." (anger)

- "I am creating a wonderful relationship with my partner/kids." (grief)
- "I am creating double my old income in the next 12 months." (lust)

3. Choose one creation to work with. Really focus on what you're feeling as you think about having it. When you've got hold of the feeling, ask yourself Lester Levenson's "releasing question": *Could I let go of wanting to change this?*

Stay with the question until you sense a release or letting go happening. If your answer is "no," ask yourself if you could let go of wanting to change your answer!

4. Every time you're able to let go of even a little bit of wanting to change, tune back in to your goal and your feelings. Carry on until you feel courageousness, acceptance, or peace in relation to it!

In a nutshell:

- Every emotion you experience is a direct response to a thought, *not* to the world around you.

- Your day doesn't create your moods; your mood creates your day.

- Urgency is nearly always a signal to slow down and/or take a break.

- Could you let go of wanting to change this?

If you're feeling desperate to move on to the next session, now would be a great time to take a little break. Slow down and smell the roses, or the cheese, or whatever it is you like to smell.

When you're feeling as though you could take it or leave it, it's probably time to begin. . . .

SESSION SIX

Have an Average Day

*"There is chaos under the heavens,
and the situation is excellent."*

— Chinese proverb

The General and the CEO

A four-star general was taking a tour of the company that had been hired by the military to complete a major defense contract.

Despite the CEO's assurance that this particular project would be completed on time, the general felt that the CEO's team was not 100 percent committed to getting the job done. He argued that they should remain at work and do "whatever it takes" to succeed, even if it meant working much longer hours, taking extra time away from home and family, and putting themselves under additional personal pressure and stress. He told the CEO that understanding personnel management was like eating bacon and eggs for breakfast: the chicken was "involved"; the pig was "committed."

The contractor smiled and said, "Well, that's true, General—but the pig is dead, and the chicken is still producing eggs. I want my people to stay 'involved.'"

The general backed down, and the project was completed on time.

In Praise of "Average"

I was talking to the supercoach Steve Chandler once when he said to me, "Have an average day!" A bit taken aback, I asked him what he meant. After all, isn't the idea to have "great" days, or even "exceptional" ones?

He then told me the story of one of his mentors, a man named Lyndon Duke, who had studied something called "the linguistics of suicide." After receiving a doctorate from two separate universities, Duke had begun analyzing suicide notes to look for linguistic clues that could be used to predict and prevent suicidal behavior in teenagers. In his research, he came across the work of Dr. Abraham Low, a contemporary of Jung and Adler who had developed his own somewhat controversial form of psychotherapy in the 1930s. Low worked with his patients to recognize that whatever unique skills or talents they might have, they were essentially human beings just like everyone else, dealing with the same problems in the best way they knew how. He called this the "average person" approach to life and contrasted it continually with what he called "the curse of exceptionality."

In a world where everyone is trying to be exceptional, two things happen. The first is that nearly everyone fails, because by definition, if too many people become exceptional, the exceptional becomes commonplace. The second is that the few who do succeed feel even more isolated and estranged from their peers than before. Consequently, you have a few people feeling envied, misunderstood, and alone and tens of thousands of others feeling like failures for not being "enough"— "good enough," "special enough," "rich enough," or even "happy enough."

This resonated deeply with my own experience. When I was in the midst of the thickest cloud of suicidal thoughts in college, I remember wishing I could run away from my Presidential scholarship and hide, perhaps changing my name to "Bob" and taking a job pumping gas at a service station somewhere in the Midwest. Only in my fantasy sooner or later people would start to notice that there was something special about me. They would begin driving miles out of their way to have their cars filled up by "Bob the service guy" and exchange a few words with him, leaving the station oddly uplifted and with a renewed sense of optimism and purpose. Before long, someone would discover how exceptional I was, and I'd have to run away from their expectations all over again. I was, to my way of thinking, doomed to succeed.

Delusions of grandeur? Quite possibly.

Depressed, hopeless, and miserable? Absolutely!

One of Lyndon Duke's major breakthroughs came when he was dealing with his own discontent and heard the sound of a neighbor singing while mowing his lawn. He realized then that despite all the "exceptional" work he was doing, what was missing from his life were the simple pleasures of an average life.

The very next weekend, he went to visit his son, who was struggling to excel in his first university term. He sat him down and told him about his revised expectations for him: "I expect you to be a straight-C student, young man. I want you to complete your unremarkable academic career, meet an ordinary young woman, and, if you choose to, get married and live a completely average life!"

His son, of course, thought Dad had finally flipped, but did take the pressure off himself to be quite so exceptional.

A month later he phoned his father to apologize. He'd gotten *A*'s on all his exams, but it was okay because he'd only done an average amount of studying.

And this is the paradoxical promise of the "average day" philosophy—the cumulative effect of a series of average days spent doing an average amount of what one loves and wants to do is actually quite extraordinary!

When I first introduce this "average day" philosophy to my clients, they sometimes freak out at the idea of "settling" for average after a lifetime of successful (or unsuccessful) overachievement. To calm their nerves, I guide them through a version of the following exercise:

One Day at a Time

1. Choose an area of your life you've been trying to excel in—for example:

- Writing
- Sales
- Being a mom

2. What would constitute an average day in that area? Not *typical*, but *average* (as in neither exceptionally good nor exceptionally bad)? For example:

- *Writing:* Spending 45 minutes a day actually writing

- *Sales:* Speaking to five new prospects

- *Being a mom:* Spending at least half an hour before and half an hour after school focused 100 percent on being with the kids

---

3. Project forward into the future—if you did nothing but repeat your "average day" five days a week, how much of a difference would you have made in three months? A year? Five years? A lifetime? For example:

— "Writing for 100 or so hours in a six-month period would probably be enough to complete an entire book; 200 hours a year would be enough to add some poetry and a screenplay. Writing more than 1,000 hours during a five-year period would make me prolific."

— "Speaking to more than 100 people a month about the difference I could make for them would definitely lead to some sales; more than 1,200 difference-making conversations a year would lead to numerous sales (and an incredible amount of skill development); more than 6,000 difference-making conversations in a five-year period would make me rich!"

— "Spending at least an hour and a half a day with my kids seven days a week would be more than 125 hours in three months, which would be more than enough time to really get to know them and tune in to their wants and needs; 500-plus focused hours of time spent with my children over the course of a year would create an incredible level of friendly intimacy and positive familiarity; if I made even a tiny difference in each one of nearly 3,000 hours over a five-year period, the impact on their lives and the sense of meaning in mine would be anything but average!"

> 4. Do three small things today that make a positive difference on a project you're working on or a direction you're moving toward. Repeat daily for as long as you like!

Slow Down to Get More Done

> *"Be quick, but don't hurry."*
>
> — John Wooden

When we take the pressure off ourselves to be exceptional—that is, be the exception to the rule—we recognize that "good enough" is nearly always good enough and that no matter how hard we try, we'll never really be able to do more than one thing at any given time.

Relax and Smile!

Whenever you're feeling that everything is spinning out of control, it's time to take a little break and slow down! Lower your standards, stop trying to be the exception to the rule that things take time and people aren't always at their best, and give yourself some space and time.

As the sign outside Logan Airport in Boston read for nearly seven years:

> *"Rome wasn't built in a day. If it had been,*
> *we would've used their contractors."*

This doesn't mean we have to always go slowly—just that when we're *willing* to slow down, we're often able to make much quicker progress on what matters most in our lives.

Several years ago, I had child psychologist and author Alfie Kohn as a guest on my radio show. At one point, I asked him if he had any tips on how to be a more caring and effective parent when you were in a hurry. His answer, tongue only slightly in cheek, was: "Don't be in a hurry."

While I laughed at the time, the more I thought about it, the more I realized what excellent advice that was, not only for parenting but for pretty much any area of our lives. When we're in a hurry, we tend to get sloppy and things are left undone or, worse still, half done. Our best intentions often go out the window and our values shift, with "expediency" and "getting stuff done" leapfrogging their way up the list above such old-fashioned priorities as "treating people with respect," "getting things right the first time," and even "enjoying the process."

Stress is a hurrier's constant companion, as there's never enough time and there's always too much to do. When time gets short, tempers get shorter, and a frayed nerve often snaps in the face of a loved one.

While you can find any number of "outside-in" approaches to getting more done with less stress (and I'll share my very favorite one at the end of the session), effective time management evolves naturally out of an understanding of the sixth secret:

No matter what seems to be going on in your life, you don't have to do anything.

"That's insane," one client told me when I first introduced this idea. "I don't know about you, but I have to go to work in the morning."

"Do you?" I responded. "What would happen if you didn't?"

"If I didn't go to work, I'd lose my job!"

Ignoring the likely fallacy of that statement, I continued, "So you choose to go to work because you want to keep your job?"

"Fair enough," he said, although he didn't look happy about it. "But I have to eat! If I don't eat, I'll die!"

"Okay," I replied. "So you choose to eat because you want to live?"

The reality is, every single thing you do or don't do is a choice. And while personally I'm a big fan of making choices that lead to things like money and food, nowadays in most cultures you don't even have to make those choices to survive. If you never got up from where you're sitting right now, someone would eventually come to check on you, if only to find out what that extraordinary smell was. And at that point, if you continued to choose not to move or feed yourself, some other people (usually dressed in white, with friendly smiles and a lot of upper-body strength) would come by and scoop you up and give you new clothes to wear and a lovely padded room to live in. They would even feed you more than enough to stay alive, although admittedly the quality of that life would be somewhat less than what you're probably accustomed to.

So the corollary to our secret ("You don't *have* to do anything") is this:

Everything that you do (or don't do) is a choice.

Given that, why would anyone ever choose to do anything they didn't want to do?

Two reasons:

1. Because they think it's necessary in order to get or maintain something that they want

2. In order to live up to an idea of how they're supposed to be in the world

In other words, we do what we do (and don't do what we don't do) either because we want to, because we think it's a prerequisite for getting something else that we want (in other words, because we "have" to), or because we think it will make us into the kind of person we're supposed to be (i.e., because we "should").

Why?

The question "Why?" gets a bad name in some coaching circles because when it's asked about anything that happened in the past, the answer is invariably a story filled with confabulations that could usefully be edited down to the phrase "Because it seemed like a good idea at the time." But when we ask the question in the present about what we're planning for the future, we quickly get an insight into our motivation.

If we hear a lot of "need to," "have to," and "must," we may have fallen into the trap of thinking there's something we have to do to survive. If there are lots of justifications and rationalizations, we're probably doing things because we think they will reinforce our self-

141

image or help us become the kind of person we "should" be. But when the answer is some variation on "Because I want to," chances are that we're following our inner wisdom.

The more quickly you can recognize the difference, the easier it will be to recognize each activity as a choice and, if you want to, choose something different.

Want to	Have to	Should
Inner guidance	Means to an end	Self-image
Choice	Prerequisite	The "right" thing
Inspiration	Desperation	Rationalization

The Strangest Discipline in the World

When I ask my clients what they think is *really* holding them back from living the life of their dreams, the most frequent answer I get is: "A lack of discipline."

When I ask them which disciplines specifically they feel they're lacking in, they tend to come back to me with some variations on these common themes:

- Thinking positive
- Taking daily action
- Doing the hard thing first
- Staying focused
- Feeling the fear and doing it anyway

While any one of the above is a worthy discipline, the practice of which will unquestionably make a positive difference to your pursuit of success, I've found that the discipline that makes the biggest difference is the strangest-sounding one of them all:

Being disciplined enough to not do what you don't want to do, even if everyone around you (and that voice inside your head) is telling you that you should.

Now at first glance this may seem like an "anti-discipline"—after all, many success primers tell us that making ourselves do what we don't want to do is the very basis of successful living. But the kind of success that's built on unhappy action is like opening an empty present—you rip off the bow, tear through the beautiful wrapping, and discover there's nothing left inside.

When you're willing to consistently not do what you don't want to do, you may find yourself:

- Doing less but accomplishing more
- Spending more time with fewer people
- Burning more brightly without burning out

This is the discipline of trusting yourself—of consistently choosing your inner knowing over outer knowledge. It's the discipline that keeps your kids from drinking or doing drugs even though their "friends" are telling them how cool it is, and that keeps you from jumping into business (or into bed) with the project or person who looks right but feels wrong.

In fact, in Marcus Buckingham's recent study of people who had made a consistent positive contribution to their fields over a period of at least 20 years, the popular management consultant and best-selling author discovered that the one common element underlying their sustained personal success was this:

*They figured out what they didn't
like doing and stopped doing it.*

I remember one journalist confronting me about this during an interview.

"It was my boyfriend's birthday last night," she began. "I didn't want to go out for the evening, but I knew he'd be really mad at me if I didn't. Are you saying I shouldn't have gone? He would have had a fit!"

I smiled at her earnestness. "Perhaps," I suggested as gently as I could, "you could begin by not doing the things you don't want to do that no one else really cares about. Sometimes it's easier when you're the only one who knows. Besides, have you ever really regretted not doing something you didn't want to do in the first place?"

While she did acknowledge the commonsense nature of my reply, there are a couple of things my clients and I have learned that make it easier to not do what you don't want to do:

1. Need less. So many of us have learned to motivate ourselves through our apparent needs. The idea that "neediness" is a more powerful motivating force than inspiration is rife in our cultural mythology. In fact, many of us have spent so many years motivating ourselves through our apparent needs that being "needy" almost feels normal. But if you want to experiment with a simpler, happier way of going for, getting, and having what you want, begin by examining how many of your "needs" are simply things you want and have promised yourself to feel bad about if you don't get.

2. Love more. While I'm not a gardener, I've been told on many occasions that if you pull up weeds but don't fill your garden with flowers, the weeds will come back. In a similar way, if you develop the discipline of not doing what you don't want to do without simultaneously doing more of what you love, you may find the same unsavory choices continuing to fill your action menu.

When you're doing what you love (and loving what you do), you'll naturally tend to engage in each of the main time-management strategies currently being touted in the marketplace:

- You'll say no to most things (because you're already doing what you love).

- You'll schedule your day (because otherwise you'd work all 24 hours).

- You'll gladly sacrifice a bit of efficiency (for the joy of getting to indulge in your passion).

- You'll get help with the stuff you don't love (so you can spend more time with what you do).

- You'll do one thing at a time (because it's so wonderful for you to take the time to do it).

Loving What You Do!

If you're not already doing what you love, choose a mundane task (washing dishes, watering plants, or something similar) and practice loving doing it.

Just as an experiment, do the task with energy and enthusiasm—as if it's the most wonderful and important thing in the world!

The Last Word on Time Management

The best time-management systems, or so it's always seemed to me, are the ones that take the least time to manage. With that in mind, I've simplified a number of the most popular examples in the marketplace into three key words—the only three things you need to do to effectively manage your time now and on into the future.

Word #1: *Clarity*

In Lewis Carroll's *Alice in Wonderland,* young Alice has the following exchange with the Cheshire Cat:

> "Would you tell me, please, which way I ought to go from here?"
>
> "That depends a good deal on where you want to get to," said the Cat.
>
> "I don't much care where—" said Alice.
>
> "Then it doesn't matter which way you go," said the Cat.

If it does matter to you which way your life goes, then the most important choice you can make is what you choose to make important.

There are a number of excellent systems for this, which I will sum up briefly:

— **ABC priorities.** This is perhaps the most common piece of time-management wisdom—prioritize your goals and tasks according to a simple ABC system of

"Must, Should, Could." My own slight variation on this is to redefine ABC in terms of real-world consequences:

A = Bad things happen if I don't.
B = Good things happen if I do.
C = That would be nice.

— **The four quadrants.** Stephen R. Covey made the four-quadrant approach of Roger and Rebecca Merrill famous in his landmark book *The 7 Habits of Highly Effective People*. Essentially, every goal or activity can be placed in one of four quadrants:

I.   Important and urgent
II. Important but not urgent
III. Not important but urgent
IV. Not important and not urgent

What makes this system different from a simple ABCD is the relative weighting of each quadrant. While Quadrant I activities (important and urgent) still need to be tackled first, the real gold is to be found in Quadrant II—doing what's important *before* it becomes urgent.

— **The 80/20 rule.** The 80/20 rule is based on an anomaly first pointed out by the 19th-century economist Vilfredo Pareto, who noticed that 80 percent of a nation's wealth seemed to be controlled by 20 percent of its people.

Once you start looking, you can find this 80/20 relationship everywhere, and time management is no exception—80 percent of your meaningful results come from 20 percent of your efforts.

The simplest way I have found to apply 80/20 to my goals and tasks is this:

1. Make up a master task list (or goal list)—
    everything you could possibly think of to do
    to move forward in your life.

2. Add up the number of items on the list and
    divide that number by 5. This will be your
    80/20 number. (For example, if there are 20
    things on the list, your 80/20 number will be
    4; if there are 50 items on your list, your 80/20
    number will be 10.)

3. Your 80/20 number represents the most
    important 20 percent of the items on your
    list. If you were only allowed to focus on this
    many goals or activities, which ones would you
    choose? Which ones would fall away?

While any of the above clarification systems are valuable, they are only necessary up to the point where you have clarity. This quality allows you to take the millions of things you could be doing with your time and narrow them down to the one, two, or three things that are really important at any given moment. It lets you choose what matters most so that it will never be at the mercy of what matters least.

But you may have noticed that even when you're clear about what's most important, you don't always manage to get it done. Enter the second word of our three-word system . . .

Word #2: *Structure*

Have you ever wondered why it is that you never find time to work on your novel or move forward on your "Wow!" goals, but you pretty much always find time to brush your teeth and take out the garbage?

Is it because teeth brushing and garbage dumping matter so much more than expressing your creativity and living the life of your dreams? Or is it because you have a structure in place for getting them done?

There are two kinds of structure that adapt most easily to getting things done effortlessly:

1. External reminders. The reason you probably get the garbage to the curb at roughly the same time each week is that you know that someone will be showing up to remove it. Knowing that your garbage gets picked up on a Wednesday morning is the surest way to make certain it gets taken out on a Tuesday night (or really, really early on Wednesday). Of course, if you forget, the smell of a week's accumulated garbage will serve as an external reminder about next week's collection.

Other useful external reminders to do something include:

- Making an appointment with another person to work on it

- Putting it in your diary as an appointment (even if it's an appointment with yourself)

- Setting an alarm to go off shortly before you're due to do it

- Leaving yourself a message about it on your answering machine

- Asking your boss, manager, colleague, friend,
  or spouse to check in with you about it and
  hold you accountable for doing it

2. Personal routine. Chances are that you almost never put "Brush teeth" on your to-do list. This is because brushing your teeth is a routine that you've followed for so long that you don't even have to think about it—you just do it.

For example, I found that when I switched from writing daily coaching tips to weekly ones, the task became much harder. My personal routine had been disrupted. Once I created a new routine, getting them done each week became so effortless that I've now written more than 700 of them!

Here are some of the traits of an effective personal routine:

- There's no decision to make—it's not based
  on whether or not you feel like it.

- It happens regularly enough that you don't
  have to remember whether or not to do it
  today.

- You've either done it or you haven't—
  there's no real wiggle room.

Which leads us to these guidelines for creating a routine:

- Tie it into an existing one, something you
  already reliably do pretty much every day.
  For example:

151

- – Practice your Italian during lunch.

- – Go for a run on the way home from the office.

- – Work on your novel in the bathroom (reportedly a favorite strategy of the French novelist Victor Hugo).

• Decide up front how much is enough. Phrases like "as long as I've written a single word," "at least ten minutes," "exactly three times," and "no more than an hour" work much better than "until I'm tired" or "as often as I can."

• Remember that the effort you put into creating the routine will be repaid in how effortless it will be to carry on with it in the future. Don't worry if it's hard to get started—you can do hard. Once you're used to it, you won't even have to think about it. It will be as natural as brushing your teeth and as easy as taking out the garbage.

Clarity of intention and value, and prioritization of tasks and projects make it easy to know what to do when; *structure,* in the form of systems, process, and routine, creates the pathways for getting those things done.

So why do we even need a third word?

Because no time-management system on Earth can get you to actually live according to your clear priorities or make use of your robust yet elegant structures.

Enter "the last word" on time management . . .

Word #3: *Boldness*

Another thing Steve Chandler pointed out to me was that ultimately, the effectiveness of any time-management system comes down to boldness—your willingness to actually follow through on your priorities and capitalize on your systems and structures, regardless of what circumstances the world happens to throw at you on any given day.

Over the years, I've worked with:

- Spouses whose partners want them home for dinner while clients want them to stay late at work

- Upwardly mobile parents trying to balance getting a raise at work with raising healthy, happy kids

- Would-be artists, musicians, and writers whose friends can seemingly never understand why they want to begin creating early in the morning when the evening's revels have only just begun

In every case, the solution to their apparent dilemma was the same: finding the boldness inside themselves to say yes to their personal priorities and no (for now) to everything else.

If you're afraid you don't have what it takes to back up your chosen priorities with action, remembering that you don't actually have to do anything will make it considerably easier. And remembering that you pretty much always see what you're looking for, chances are that if you look around a bit, you'll probably find loads of places where you're already a shining example of boldness in action.

For example, how often do you miss a flight when you're going on vacation? Do you think you would turn up late to a meeting with your child's doctor about their mystery illness? When's the last time you missed out on great sex because "something came up"?

The reason why there are certain things in your life that you can always find time for is because you hold them in a different way in your brain. Instead of thinking of them as things you'll do "if possible" or "circumstances permitting," you look upon them as things you'll get done "or die trying."

And while there's no point in running yourself ragged trying to live up to the countless expectations people attempt to dump on you throughout a typical day, isn't it nice to know that if the commitment you've made is to your own success, happiness, and well-being, you're more than capable of keeping it?

What If It <u>Really</u> Isn't Up to Me?

Are there circumstances that really do make it impossible to follow through on your priorities on any given day? Sometimes.

No matter how much you want to get to work on time, if your car explodes, the buses aren't running, the roads are closed, and there are armed police officers in the streets picking off the cyclists and joggers, it might be worth waiting around for a few hours until things get a little less frantic. But in all honesty, when was the last time you really found yourself in that situation?

In my book *You Can Have What You Want,* I offer what I call the "million-dollar question": *If you knew that you were going to be paid a million dollars (or whatever would be exciting and inspirational for you) for the successful achievement of whatever it is you say you want in your life, what would you do differently to go about getting it?*

If you can answer this question, you know that the problem isn't outside you, it lies in a lack of clarity about what there is to be done, a lack of structure to support you in doing it, or a lack of boldness to follow through on what matters most to you.

And, fortunately for all of us, clarity, structure, and boldness are never more than a thought and an action away.

I promised that I would share my favorite time-management technique with you before the end of our session. This is another Steve Chandler special. Here's all you need to do:

The Ultimate Time-Management System

1. Get two pieces of paper. (I like to use the top two pages of a Post-it pad, but it really doesn't matter!)

2. On the first page, write the words "**The only thing I have to do today is . . .**"

3. On the second page, make a fairly comprehensive to-do list—anything you can think of that you want to get done in the next week or so.

4. When it's time to begin working through your list, choose one item to work on first. Rewrite it on the first page. For example:

   The only thing I have to do today is . . .
   finish reading this journal article.

5. Actually do whatever you've written down as if it's the only thing you have to do today.

6. When you complete that item, cross it off on both lists and repeat Steps 4 to 6.

In a nutshell:

- Being overwhelmed is just a thought.

- No matter what seems to be going on in your life, you don't *have* to do anything.

- Everything you do (or don't do) is a choice.

- When in doubt, slow down.

- Clarity, structure, and boldness underpin every time-management system in the world.

You may find that over the course of a day you do a bit less and take a bit longer than usual, but paradoxically you'll get more done and have more fun doing it.

Have fun, learn heaps, and when the only thing you have to do today is move on to the next session, I'll see you there!

SESSION SEVEN

Listening Made Fun

"I honor the place in you where the entire universe resides. I honor the place in you of love, of truth, of peace, and of light. And when you are in that place in you and I am in that place in me, there is only one of us."

— a definition of the word *Namaste*

Vaudeville

Fred: *Hey, George? I say, I say, is that you, George?*

George: *Why, hello, Fred!*

Fred: *I say, George, did you know that you have a banana in your ear?*

George: [loudly] *What was that, Fred?*

Fred: *I said, you have a banana in your ear, George. A great big yellow banana right there in your ear.*

George: [even louder] *What are you saying, Fred?*

Fred: [yelling] *WILL YOU PLEASE TAKE THAT BANANA OUT OF YOUR EAR, GEORGE!*

George: [yelling back] *I'M SORRY, FRED, BUT YOU'LL HAVE TO SPEAK A LITTLE LOUDER! I CAN'T HEAR YOU—I HAVE A BANANA IN MY EAR!*

❖

Creative Listening

Listening is a deceptive skill, mostly because it seems as if there's no skill involved at all. But when it comes to our relationships with other people, it's perhaps the most important skill of all. The secret we'll be exploring in this session is this:

We create other people by how we listen to them.

Now I obviously don't mean this literally—I've only actually created three little people in this lifetime, and it wasn't by listening! But in the same way that we'll almost always see what we're looking for, we'll nearly always hear what we're listening for.

This creates a self-fulfilling prophecy within all our relationships. If I'm listening for my lover, I'm sure to hear her; if I'm listening for that harridan of a wife, I'll hear her, too. Listen for your loving son and he's bound to respond; listen for that irresponsible young man and sure enough, he's there.

This works because our relationships with other people happen almost entirely in our heads. Remember that when you think about people, you aren't actually thinking about the "real" them—you're thinking about a representation of them in your mind, like an icon on a computer. You're actually re-creating them in your mind; and you're deleting, distorting, and generalizing some of their characteristics as you do so.

At some point, we decide what people are *really* like, and from that moment on, we maintain them in our minds as a fixed persona. We listen for the person we expect to hear and filter out anything that doesn't fit with the character we've created for that individual.

"So you're saying that I'm creating my husband as a miserable, moody, self-righteous pain in the ass?" one woman asked me.

"Absolutely," I replied, channeling my inner Dr. Phil. "How's that working out for you?"

When it comes to enjoying great relationships, the thing to remember is this:

There are four of you in every couple, and
two of you are really in the way.

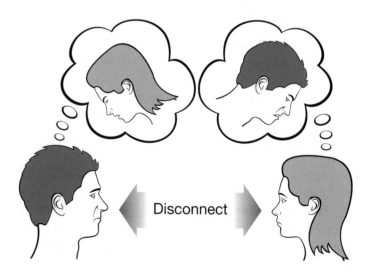

How to Connect

There's a famous story about Marilyn Monroe (born Norma Jeane Mortenson) walking in New York City with a friend. When her friend commented on how wonderful it was that she was able to maintain her anonymity in public, Marilyn said, "That's because I am walking as

Norma Jeane. If I walked as Marilyn, everyone would notice me."

Her friend, disbelieving, encouraged her to show her what she meant. At that moment, Norma Jeane transformed herself into Marilyn Monroe, the movie star. An energy began to radiate from her, and within minutes she was surrounded by autograph-seeking fans.

So what happened? What was the seemingly magical shift that turned an anonymous woman into a movie star in a matter of moments?

Patsy Rodenburg is a voice coach and acting teacher who, along with working with the Royal Shakespeare Company and Royal National Theatre in London, taught voice while I was in the professional-actor training program at Southern Methodist University in Texas. In her book *The Second Circle,* she describes this phenomenon in relation to three circles (she deliberately outlines the first and third before the second):

— The **First Circle** is the circle of introspection— the place where your energy barely extends beyond the bounds of your own body. In this circle, your focus is inward, and you're most likely to be "lost in thought," listening to that voice inside your head even while life is going on around you.

— The **Third Circle** is the circle of aggression—the place where your energy becomes a weapon used to charm, bully, or otherwise impose your will onto those around you. It also serves as a shield, creating a moat around the castle of your being that is often impenetrable even by those you wish to invite inside.

— The **Second Circle** is the circle of connection—
your energy goes out but also comes back in. This is the
circle of "being with." Whatever you're truly connected
to is what you're present to, and if this is another human
being or group of human beings, they'll be as fascinated
by your very presence as you'll become by theirs.

I experience this all the time with audiences when
I teach—I somehow manage to fall in love with a room
full of strangers simply because I'm "being with" them
in as naked and honest a way as I know how to be. When
I don't—either because I'm too nervous or too confident
or too distracted—I can still bluster my way through
a talk in "Third Circle," but the intimacy, magic, and
connection are lost. Speaking becomes a job, and while
an audience may still enjoy what I have to say, their
experience of what I have to offer will be a considerably
more limited one.

It is this quality of connection that makes romantic
love so intoxicating and allows new parents to stare into
their babies' eyes for hours on end. To simply be with
someone or something in a state of full presence is one
of the most magical gifts we're given in our lives, and
one that for most of us is under-received because we
think we play no part in its arrival.

To connect more fully, try this exercise, which is
based on the work of supercoach Lee Glickstein:

Being With

1. Take a few moments to center yourself. You may want to take three slow and gentle breaths with your eyes closed and simply be with yourself.

2. Now open your eyes and choose any object in the space you're currently in. Take a minute or so to "be with" that object—that is, allow yourself to become fully present to it, as if it were the most important thing in the world.

One way to do this is through what Patsy Rodenburg calls "breathing to it." Imagine that you're reaching out directly to the object with your breath. When you get the hang of this, you'll feel a sense of being completely present with it—as though you and the object are connected in some way.

3. When you're familiar with what it feels like to "be with" an object, try it with a friend (or in a pinch, a beloved pet!). Just take a couple of moments to center yourself, and then simply "be with" one another, without words and without effort. Don't worry if it feels awkward or uncomfortable at first—you'll get past that, and the sweet feeling of connection you'll get to will be completely worth it!

4. Finally, allow yourself to experiment with what it's like to "be with" the rest of the people who are in your world. There's no formal exercise here— as you get used to being fully present with others, it will naturally begin to infuse your relationships and enhance your presence in the world.

Of course, you don't have to "be with" everyone—but isn't it nice to know that you could?

Learn to Listen, Listen to Learn

". . . and words are dangerous, because you might listen to them. And that would be a mistake."

— Ram Dass

One of the things I challenge coaches on my "Coaching Mastery" intensives to do is to become conscious of their unconscious assumptions, filters, and habits and how each of those aspects of the coaching process impacts the results they're able to produce with their clients. In particular, I ask them to become aware of *how* they habitually listen, whether they're listening to their clients, their teachers, their colleagues, their children, or even themselves.

Here are three of the most common distinctions people make:

1. Listening For vs. Listening To

There's an old joke about a therapist who operated on the theory that all problems could be traced to dreaming about fish. A patient came to him complaining about his lackluster sexual relations with his wife. Here's a transcript of their first session together:

Patient: My wife and I just aren't getting along, doctor, you know, in bed. Between my work schedule and her dealing with the kids, it just feels as if the magic's gone.

Therapist: Hmm . . . tell me, do you ever dream?

P: Uh—sure I dream.

T: Tell me your most recent dream.

P: Well, I don't remember much. I was walking down a city street, and there were lots of tall buildings and cars but no people.

T: Had it been raining?

P: Not sure—I guess it might have been.

T: So there were puddles?

P: I suppose there could have been puddles.

T: And, I'm just guessing here, might there have been fish in those puddles?

P: Wow—I suppose there might have been . . .

T: [triumphant] Aha! Just as I suspected—fish in the dreams!

While most of our own biases aren't so obvious and don't seem so silly (at least to us), the point is that if you're listening for something specific, you'll tend to find it. Listen for hesitation in the voice of your partner and—boom!—you've "caught" your mate lying to you. Listen for warning signs of trouble in your relationship and before you know it, they'll be everywhere.

The problem doesn't so much have to do with what you're listening for, but what you'll miss by listening for it. Whether it's the affection in your partner's voice, the look of love in their eyes, or the sadness in your child's heart when they're telling you about what happened at school today, if you're looking too hard for something else, you're liable to miss what's actually there. But as soon as you expand your listening palette, you'll be able to hear more and more.

That's not to say you must never listen for anything. One of the filters I've found quite useful as a coach is to listen to language literally—that is, to take what others say as a literal representation of what is going on in their minds. For example, I remember a client telling me that he felt as though his debts were pressing in on him, and his finances were so tight that at times he found it difficult to breathe. I asked him to briefly visualize his finances and notice where in his internal world he "saw" them. Sure enough, his pictures were 360-degree wraparound panoramas surrounding him and literally "pressing up against him."

When I asked him to unwrap the panorama and lay it out on the floor beneath him, he immediately began to breathe more easily. When he shrank it down to the size of one sheet of paper, he seemed like a different person. He became quiet for a few moments and then said, "Oh, is that it? I can handle that." Like the traveler who discovers in a flash of lightning that the "snake" he's hiding from is just a piece of coiled-up rope, by changing his pictures he was able to give himself a new and empowered perspective on his problems.

Here are some of the most useful patterns that come up again and again in my work:

- **"I just can't see myself doing that."** Taken literally, that means you can't make an internal movie or picture of yourself doing whatever is being discussed. Once you *can* create that internal imagery, you'll often find it easier to move forward.

- **"This is a *big* problem for me."** If you shrink down your internal representation of the situation, does it still seem so big? If you make it smaller and smaller, does it still seem like a problem?

- **"I'm stuck."** How do you know you're stuck? On what? With what? What do you want to use to unstick yourself? Which parts of your life/work/relationship are flowing? If you increase that flow, would that be enough to unstick you?

- **"The future looks bleak."** What happens if you brighten it up? Make your internal images big and bold. Drop in some pictures of things you would love to see happen . . . and see what happens!

- **"I'm hanging on by a thread here."**
  Interwoven steel thread is actually remarkably strong. And if you tie it onto your waist and engage fully with your challenges, you just might find you enjoy the climb. . . .

Here are some simple exercises you can use to play with this on your own:

Listen to Language Literally

1. Go through each of the preceding examples and actually try them on with real situations in your life.

a. Is there anything you can't see yourself doing that you might like to do? Go ahead and make a mental movie of yourself doing it until it seems "normal" and "natural."

b. Are there any big problems in your life? Shrink them down and notice what new ideas come to mind!

2. Just for fun, listen to language literally this week. Notice how many times others are telling you exactly what is going on in their internal world.

3. If you're up for a more interactive challenge, ask people what they're seeing in their minds in relation to what they're saying to you out loud.
   While some people will wonder what you mean, most will simply tell you exactly how they're representing their world inside their heads.

---

2. Listening to the Voice Inside Your Head vs. Listening to the Other Person

Have you ever had your best "Go ahead, I'm listening" face on while inside your head you're saying to yourself something like: "Oh my God, I can't believe he's telling me this for the nine-millionth time. Will he ever learn? What day is it today? Is it Tuesday? I wonder if there'll be something good on television tonight . . . ?"

As you may have noticed, when we get caught up in our internal dialogue, we not only lose track of what another person is saying to us, we often lose the plot altogether. Yet most of us habitually go inside our heads while "listening" in order to formulate our response to what's being said. This is roughly akin to looking for your keys inside the house instead of out in the street because the lighting's better indoors. But if the keys are outside, you won't find them on the inside, no matter how well illuminated things may appear.

While this may seem harmless enough in the moment, when it becomes habitual, it can be the beginning of the end for a great many relationships, both business and personal.

For example, I was once having a discussion with a potential client who was struggling with her husband's lack of emotional availability. While she didn't want to get a divorce, she also didn't want to have to, as she put it, "live with an emotional corpse" for the rest of her life.

She was explaining all the ways in which her husband's lack of emotional intelligence manifested itself when I stopped her.

"You sound like a trial lawyer making her closing argument," I said.

"Actually, that was just my opening argument!" she replied.

I laughed, but she didn't, so I asked her if she'd ever come across the popular relationship book for women called *The Rules*.

"I think so," she said. "Wasn't that the one that told you how many days to wait before phoning a guy back, when not to say 'I love you,' and things like that?"

"That's the one," I said. "There's also one for guys called *The Game*, which claims to lay out the way for men to get around the rules. The problem with both of those books, and in fact any system that claims to teach you how to 'win the game of love,' is this: *when it comes to relationships, if you're playing to win, you've already lost*. The same thing is true here. It doesn't matter how good a 'case' you can build against your husband—if you keep putting your partner on trial, you may win the arguments, but you'll ultimately lose the relationship."

Something about the directness of that seemed to strike her, and her voice softened as she asked me, "So how am I supposed to stop doing it?"

"That's the beauty of it," I pointed out. "You don't have to. All you have to do is recognize when it's happening and not take it so seriously. It will pass, and before you know it you'll be right back to the heart of any relationship—the deep feeling of love, connection, and well-being that makes being in a long-term committed relationship so wonderful."

She thought about that for a few moments and then asked with a smile in her voice, "But what if I have a really strong case?"

This time we both laughed, and I pointed out that in relation to our thinking, we have a choice:

We can entertain our thoughts about others,
or we can allow our thoughts about others to entertain us.

Here are a couple of things you can do to begin to enjoy your habitual thoughts instead of being distracted by them:

1. Imagine you're actually about to enter into a courtroom to "make the case" against the person you're having trouble with. How have they wronged you? In what ways have you been maligned and misunderstood? Play with turning up the heat on your case until it begins to sound like a country-music song. You'll know you've cranked it up enough when it begins to make you smile instead of scowl.

2. Notice what happens to your experience when you recognize that it's not the other person but your *thoughts* about that other person that are driving you nuts!

3. Listening Hard vs. Listening Easy

"Purpose tremor" is a phrase that describes the slight shake most people notice in their hands when they first try to thread a needle or remove the shinbone in a game of *Operation*. Simply put, our muscles work better when we're not trying so hard to *make* them work better.

What's sometimes less obvious is that the same thing is true with our listening:

It's easier to hear what's really going on with other people
when we're not trying so hard to listen to them.

When you listen to another person speaking in the way you might listen to pleasant background music (the kind they play on "easy listening" stations), things will often jump out at you that turn out to be the keys to unlocking whatever is going on for that person.

And when you learn to listen to yourself in the same way, it becomes easier and easier to separate out your own mental chatter from the still, small voice of wisdom within.

How do you do it?

Easy Listening

1. Choose a few non-crucial conversations to experiment with this week and notice what you can about your own habitual listening filters. Are you listening for problems or opportunities? Holes in other people's argument or openings for resolution? What they're saying with their words or what they're communicating with their feelings?

2. Just for this week, try turning down the volume on the voice inside your head when you're listening to someone else speak. Notice how much more you hear and whether or not this actually does make the other person feel "heard."

3. Practice "easy listening" this week—listening the way a tape recorder might do it. There's no effort involved—just allow the words to come in and pass right through you, with nothing on your mind and no agenda as to what you do or don't want to hear.

Would You Listen to Yourself?

Practice "easy listening" to your own internal dialogue this week and discover . . . what you can discover.

In a nutshell:

- We create other people by how we listen to them.

- When it comes to relationships, if you're playing to win, you've already lost.

- You can entertain your thoughts about others, or you can let your thoughts about others entertain you.

When you're ready, I'll be waiting for you in the very next session. . . .

How to Ask for Anything from Anyone

"If I had a prayer, it would be this: 'God, spare me from the desire for love, approval, or appreciation. Amen.'"

— Byron Katie

The Cookie Thief

A young woman was early to catch her flight home for the holidays when she decided to get herself a snack. The smell of fresh-baked cookies caught her attention, and she bought a bag full of them to help pass the time while she waited.

Although the airport was overflowing with people, a kindly looking gentleman made space for her next to him, and she gratefully sat down. After a few moments, she reached her hand down into the bag and pulled out the first of her afternoon treats. To her surprise, the "gentleman" reached into the bag just moments later and took one of the cookies for himself.

Shocked by this rude behavior, she decided to be the bigger person and not say a word. Looking around to see if anyone had noticed, she took a second cookie out of the bag, determined to savor it. But before she had even finished the first bite, the man once again reached into the bag and took another cookie for himself. Although she did little to disguise her displeasure, she was still shocked into silence by the boldness of his action.

This cookie thievery went on for the next few minutes like a game of tennis, with first her hand and then the stranger's dipping into the bag one after the other until there was only one cookie left.

"Surely he wouldn't take the last cookie," she thought. He wouldn't dare. Would he?

But no sooner had she thought the thought than the man's hand dipped into the very bottom of the bag and came out with the very last, delectable cookie.

To her amazement, the man actually smiled at her as he broke the cookie in half, handing her the larger of the two halves as he left his seat to dispose of the cookie bag and no doubt find some other unsuspecting young woman to take advantage of.

Just then her flight was called. As she stood up to get in line to board the plane, still shaking with anger at the actions of the stranger, she noticed to her dismay a full bag of cookies, still sitting on the ground by her feet where she'd left them.

◆

The "Need" for Approval

Steve Hardison is a somewhat legendary figure in the coaching world, not only for his incredible effectiveness as a supercoach but also for the jaw-dropping fees he charges and his ability to ask pretty much anyone for pretty much anything.

One of my favorite stories about him dates back to his time as a missionary for the Mormon church. One time Steve had gone up to a house and had begun speaking about the church's teachings to a man who answered the door. No doubt he had experienced doors being slammed many times over the years, but this man went a step further and actually punched him in the face. Steve's nose began to bleed, but without missing a beat, he asked the man for a towel to help stop the bleeding so they could continue their conversation.

What is it that allows one person to ask and ask and ask for what he wants, while others stop themselves before even popping the very first question?

This is the simple secret at the heart of this session:

**You can ask anyone for anything
when you make it okay for them to say "no."**

Your ability to not take the word *no* personally, no matter how dramatically that "no" may be delivered, is the key to success—not (by definition) because people will always say yes, but because it won't be emotionally devastating to you if they don't. The more comfortable you get with the word *no,* the less likely you are to get caught up in a sort of "post-traumatic stress disorder" of the mind, walking on eggshells and becoming more and more afraid to ask for what you want.

One of the things that can make it considerably easier to face up to the possibility of a strong "no" is knowing that this response invariably comes from one of three places:

1. Other people's fear that you will "make" them hear something they don't want to hear or do something they don't want to do

2. A lack of information or understanding about how what you're asking will be of benefit to them, either directly or indirectly

3. A genuine awareness on their part that they don't want to be, do, or have what you're requesting

If their response is coming from fear, you don't have to take it personally because it's about their internal state, not you or your external request.

If it's coming from a lack of information, it's still impersonal—it's up to you whether or not to continue until they have enough information to make an informed decision.

If they're saying no because they really don't want to, that's still nothing to do with you—it's simply a statement from them to them about their willingness to trust their own intuition, awareness, and inner knowing.

So why do we take "no" so personally?

Because when we make our requests, we tend to put our self-image and self-esteem and even physical survival on the line along with whatever it is we're requesting. Instead of simply asking for the sale, the job, or the hand in marriage, our self-directed subtext gets rolled into the question and what we're actually asking goes a little something like this:

> "Would you please do as I'm requesting *and* approve of me, affirm me as a human being, ensure I have whatever I need to survive, and let me know I'm worthy of your acceptance?"

That's a tall order for anyone, let alone someone you've never met before!

In fact, one of the simplest ways to overcome the fear of asking for what you want is to notice whether your attention is on you or the person you're asking. If it's on you—your self-image, self-worth, or what it might mean to you for them to say "yes" or "no" to your request—you'll inevitably feel fear or discomfort. But the moment you turn the full light of your attention onto the other person and how what you're asking will benefit and serve that individual, the discomfort disappears and you'll find it surprisingly easy to ask for what you want.

In order to see how the desire for approval serves as an obstacle to asking for what you want, consider going up to 100 people and either asking for something you want or selling them a product or your own services. Now, 50 of these people already know you very well—they're members of your family or friends and colleagues. The other 50 are complete strangers and don't know anything about you.

Which group would you find it easier to approach?

In my experience, people are fairly split in their answers to this question, but fewer than 5 in 100 would find approaching *both* groups to ask for what they want or sell their product or services an effortless, fun endeavor.

The reason is that we don't want to risk the disapproval of others, not even complete strangers. But imagine how much easier it would be to ask for what you wanted if your sense of well-being were strong enough for you not to worry about what other people thought of you in order to feel safe, happy, and well.

In other words, the desire for approval is really the desire for safety and well-being, and it can never be found if we continue to look for it in the wrong place—outside our innermost selves.

As we discussed in Session Two, all happiness, well-being, and wisdom come from within. They aren't the fruit of something you do; they're the essence of who you are. And there's nothing you can ask for and be given from the outside that will fill the hole you've been digging for yourself on the inside.

Who Do You Think They Are?

> "In America everybody is of the opinion that he has
> no social superiors, since all men are equal, but he
> does not admit that he has no social inferiors."
>
> — Bertrand Russell

Of course, another thing that triggers our "need for approval" thoughts is believing that we are in some way less than the person of whom we're making our request.

For example, I was checking into a hotel once and found myself stuck behind someone who was trying to get an upgrade by intimidating the woman behind the desk.

"You'd better be careful, lady," our irritated asker said, "or I'll tell you who I am!"

While I have no idea who he was, the point is that people who are caught up in their insecure thinking about asking will often resort to status, real or imagined, as a way of compensating for their own discomfort.

How to Ask

The best book I've ever read on the power of asking to get what you want is Jack Canfield and Mark Victor Hansen's *The Aladdin Factor*. In it, they offer the following eight suggestions for how to ask:

1. Ask as if you expect to get it.

2. Ask someone who can give it to you.

3. Be clear and specific in your requests.

4. Ask with humor and creativity.

5. Ask from the heart.

6. Be prepared to give something in order to get something.

7. Ask repeatedly.

8. Be gracious in accepting a "no."

One of my clients was trying to understand why she felt nervous with certain people but completely confident with others. After exploring and discarding numerous theories, we soon found it clear that the pattern was as follows:

- If she felt someone was "better" than she was in some way, she felt nervous.

- If she felt someone was "a bit beneath" her in some way, she felt confident.

In an impromptu and extraordinarily unscientific poll I then conducted among my friends, these were the top ten reasons (in no particular order) for feeling superior or inferior to a fellow human being:

1. Being larger or smaller in height or weight

2. Being physically stronger or weaker

3. Having a degree or qualification from a better or lesser school

4. Being older or younger

5. Being more or less experienced

6. Being more or less of an "expert"

7. Being more or less beautiful/handsome

8. Achieving a higher or lower level of "success"

9. Earning more or less money

10. Doing more or fewer "good" works in the world

So how do you feel better in relation to someone who you think is in some way better than you?

One piece of advice I've heard given to both salespeople and public speakers is that if you feel frightened when you're about to speak to an individual or a group, imagine them in their underwear or sitting on the toilet. (This does make people seem less imposing, but I've always found it kind of gross!)

An early mentor, Stuart Wilde, taught me a similar trick—to imagine myself 30 feet tall, towering over the "puny people" in the audience. Dr. Richard Bandler, the creator of Neuro-Linguistic Programming (NLP), teaches his students to imagine themselves inside the body of a sleek black puma, looking out at the world through bright yellow eyes and saying to themselves, "Your ass is mine!"

The problem with all these "humanizing" games is that while they do often result in reduced nerves, they tend to also result in dehumanizing the people we play them with. In fact, it's not at all uncommon to see a speaker with supreme self-confidence come off as simply arrogant. They might feel great, but their audience won't care—they won't feel connected, or in some cases even acknowledged. My feeling is that if you're going to imagine others in their underwear, do it because you find them attractive!

Although psychologist Alfred Adler once quipped, "To be human means to feel inferior," making a shift from feeling inferior to superior is simply trading one way of denying our shared humanity for a slightly more pleasant one.

A third option, and the one I proposed to my client, is to cultivate a sense of "unique equality"—a recognition of both your uniqueness and your commonality with every person on the planet. (If you're wondering what you have in common with the most horrible people you can imagine, it's this: you're both doing the best you can based on your beliefs and values to move toward happiness and away from sorrow, and you're both going to die one day. As George Bernard Shaw said, "Be patient with the poor people who . . . think they will live for ever, which makes death a division instead of a bond.")

When you see the people around you as being both unique *and* "just like you"—no better and no worse—you open up the gateway to more love, deeper connection, and longer-lasting relationships. You may not feel as "confident" as you would if you held yourself to be superior, but you'll get to feel something even better— an ongoing sense of ease and well-being, regardless of whom you happen to be with.

Here's an experiment that will bring this experience home to you:

A Unique Equality

1. Make a list of three people—one you look up to, one you see as an equal, and one you suspect might be a little bit beneath you. (Obviously you're too enlightened to really think someone is beneath you, but if you did, who would it be? Someone in the office who gossips? Your least favorite politician? The local drunk outside the convenience store?)

2. Now, go inside and notice *how* you think about these people. Where in your mind do you "see" them? Are they above you, below you, or at eye level? To the

---

left, to the right, or directly in front of you? Are you seeing them through your own eyes, or do you see yourself in the picture with them?

3. Play around with each image. Notice what happens if you lift the first person up above you so you have to literally "look up" at them. How do you feel? Do you feel more or less comfortable in their virtual presence? What do you think about this person as you look up at them?

4. Next, put the person beneath you so you're literally "looking down" on them. How do you feel? Do you feel more or less powerful? What do you think about this person as you look at them "down there"?

5. Finally, see the person directly in front of you, so you can look each other straight in the eye. Notice how you feel. Do you feel more or less comfortable? More or less powerful? What do you think about this person as you look directly at them?

6. Repeat Steps 2 to 5 for the other two people on your list. Notice where you have them sorted in your internal hierarchy, and decide where you'd like to put them from now on.

7. Take each of the three people you have been thinking about (and anyone else you know!) and put their name into the following sentences. Notice whatever feelings come up as you say each one, either inside your head or aloud:

a. "I am better than _____."
b. "_____ is better than me."
c. "I am _____'s equal."
d. "_____ is my equal."

Over the Edge of the World

As I mentioned, one of my first mentors was Stuart Wilde. As well as being an author, Stuart delights in taking people out to the edges of their thought-created world and, on occasion, pushing them over the edge and out into a larger world of fresh experiences and new possibilities.

In fact, one of the reasons you're reading this now is because Stuart pushed me. Before I'd ever run a training on my own, he asked me to go out in front of a group of people to lead a "trust fall" as part of his "Warrior's Wisdom" course.

For those of you who haven't done one before, a trust fall is where a group of people who don't know each other very well have to catch one another as they fall backward blindfolded off a table, a ladder, or in our case an eight-foot-high tree stump. If the group learns to work together quickly, no one gets hurt and everybody learns about the power of trust. If people don't learn to work together quickly, people do get hurt and everybody learns something else.

Totally terrified by my insecure thoughts about being placed in the role of both "teacher" and "coach" for the first time, I asked Stuart what I was supposed to do. He said, "It's a trust fall—trust!"

To make a long story short, I trusted, they fell, and 20 years later I'm still working with individuals and standing up in front of groups, a testament to the catalyzing power of being willing to follow a trusted guide out over the edge of your world (something we'll talk about further in Session Ten).

In my years of coaching and teaching since that day, I've learned a number of other exercises and experiments that will take you out to the edges of your world and invite you to step out over that edge—into uncharted waters filled with at least one mermaid for every dragon and at least one new rise for every fall. These experiments range from the gentle to the extreme—but remember, the only real obstacle to moving forward is a thought about what might happen if you do. . . .

To get started, I recommend you begin here:

For the next 30 days, make at least one "unreasonable" request per day.

A request counts as "unreasonable" if you can't think of any reason for the person to say "yes." As you go through this process, you may be surprised by how reasonable many of your seemingly unreasonable requests turn out to be.

Over the Edge of the World

Here are some other ways to go over the edge of your world:

1. If you're someone who is habitually argumentative, seek out someone you fundamentally disagree with and have a conversation where you completely agree with everything they say. If you're generally more of a "go along to get along" type, find someone you like and get into an argument with them!

2. Go into work tomorrow dressed completely differently from the way you normally dress. (Stuart used to recommend a chicken costume. . . .) If anyone comments, just smile and go about your business.

3. Make a list of "forbidden" words—ones you would never even think of using in polite company. Choose a different word for each of the next seven days and work it into your conversations as often as you can.

4. Go to a place of business and deliberately ask for a product or service you know they don't provide. Order a pizza in a Chinese restaurant. Walk into a clothing store

and ask them to repair your vacuum cleaner. No matter how they react, stick with your request until you're ready to leave.

5. Choose a store you've never been to before. Pick an item off the shelf, go to the checkout, and offer 10 percent of the asking price in cash—$1 for a $10 book, $50 for a $500 television set, and so on.

Here's a simple exercise I teach my clients that will help you prepare for any request you want to put forth without taking things personally:

The Circle

1. Imagine you're sitting at the very center of a circle.

2. Now, imagine that all the people who love and care for you are taking their places in that circle and are looking directly at you in a loving way. Don't limit yourself to "reality"—your circle can include people from your past, present, and future; it can include pets, characters from books and movies, and even divine beings. Keep filling the circle until you feel almost overwhelmed by an absolute knowing that no matter what you do or don't do, you're loved exactly the way that you are.

3. When you're ready, imagine someone you want to make a request of standing outside the circle. Continue to feel the love and care of your circle as you ask the person for what you want, from them and for them.

Once you've had the experience of being safely inside, there are a number of fun ways of making use of the circle to recondition your thinking about how easy it can be to ask for what you want:

- From within your circle, imagine the person says "no" out of fear that you'll somehow "make" them do something. Can you see the fear? How else could you respond to put them at ease?

- Now, imagine them saying "no" because they don't have enough information. What could you do to make sure they really know how much what you're asking will do for them, directly or indirectly?

- Imagine they're saying "no" because they simply don't want to. What would it be like to just thank them for listening and move on to the next person?

- Tune back in to the loving faces and energy in your circle until you can hear that "no" and know it can't harm you in any way, shape, or form. Then imagine yourself asking person after person again and again until some begin to enthusiastically say "yes" to your request!

- What's the worst thing you can imagine someone saying or doing in response to your request? Is it punching you in the face? Shouting at you? Pointing at you and laughing and whispering to their friends? Whatever it is, connect with the energy of your circle and watch them do what they do, knowing that it has nothing to do with you and everything to do with their own unhappiness, confusion, and misunderstanding.

- Finally, imagine the person you're asking saying an enthusiastic "Yes!" to your request. Notice that even though you're pleased with this response, the feeling of connection with your circle is an even deeper, more wonderful feeling than the pleasure of the "yes."

Take your circle with you into the world. Tune back in to it in the moments before you approach anyone about anything until you know that no matter what happens, you are safe, valued, and loved.

And of course, if you want me there, I look forward to seeing you in your circle!

In a nutshell:

- You can ask anyone for anything when you make it okay for them to say "no."

- A "no" is never about you, even if the other person thinks it is.

- When you see the people around you as being both unique and "just like you"—no better and no worse—you open up the gateway to more love, deeper connection, and longer-lasting relationships.

- When you meet your own need for approval, you never have to fear rejection.

The next time you're deciding on a course of action that involves at least one other person, try asking yourself the following question first:

If I already had all the love in the world, how would I do this differently?

199

Have fun, learn heaps, and meet me in the next session when you're ready!

The Secret to a Lifetime of Financial Security

"[Security] does not exist in nature, nor do the children of men as a whole experience it. . . . Avoiding danger is no safer in the long run than outright exposure. . . . Life is either a daring adventure or nothing."

— Helen Keller

The Rich Man and the Beggar

Many years ago, a man was sitting in quiet contemplation by a riverbank when he was disturbed by a beggar from the local village.

"Where is the stone?" the beggar demanded. "I must have the precious stone!"

The man smiled up at him. "What stone do you seek?"

"I had a dream," the beggar answered, barely able to slow his words enough to speak, "and in that dream a voice told me that if I went to the riverbank, I would find a man who would give me a precious stone that would end my poverty forever!"

The man looked thoughtful, then reached into his bag and pulled out a large diamond.

"I wonder if this is the stone." he said kindly. "I found it on the path. If you'd like it, you may certainly have it."

The beggar couldn't believe his luck, and he snatched the stone and ran back to the village before the man could change his mind.

One year later, the beggar, now dressed in the clothes of a wealthy man, came back to the riverbank in search of his anonymous benefactor.

"You have returned, my friend!" said the man, who was again sitting in his favorite spot enjoying the peaceful flow of the water before him. "What has happened?"

The beggar humbled himself before the man.

"Many wonderful things have happened to me because of the diamond you gave me so graciously. I have become wealthy, found a wife, and bought a home. I am now able to give employment to others and to do what I want, when I want, with whomever I want."

"So why have you returned?" asked the man.

"Please," the beggar said. "Teach me whatever it is inside you that allowed you to give me that stone so freely."

The $600 Million Man

When I first began working with high-income/high-net-worth clients, I was surprised that money came up so frequently as an issue. Men and women with six-figure incomes and millions in the bank were dealing with the same kinds of fears and concerns around their finances as the people I knew with no money in the bank and no income to speak of.

I would often hear phrases like:

- "I don't want to, but I need the money."
- "With the economy the way it is, I don't know how I'm ever going to be able to retire."
- "I have to worry—otherwise I might lose it all!"

Apparently, having a high income or a huge bank balance had little or no impact on feeling secure about money. I actually found this quite disconcerting. I had somehow convinced myself that there was a magic number and that once my bank balance hit it, I would never have to worry about money again.

What finally completely divested me of that illusion was when one client whose net worth was nearly $600 million told me that he woke up every morning wondering if today was going to be the day he lost it all. It finally got through to me that if $600 million wasn't enough to guarantee financial security, $600 billion wouldn't be enough either (and neither would $600,000 or $100,000 or whatever other number had seemed to my brain at the time to be more money than I could possibly spend in a lifetime).

I remember making a little note to keep by my desk that read:

My well-being is not dependent on my bank balance.

This phenomenon quite clearly worked in both directions. At the same time that I was working with my insecure millionaires, I had other clients who had far less money in the bank but didn't seem to worry about it at all.

As always, the difference between financial security and financial insecurity was being created from the inside out.

To understand what does lead to financial security, imagine this scenario:

> You live in a cold climate. Your partner asks you to put some more wood on the fire, but when you look in the woodpile, it's almost empty. What do you do next?

If you're like most people, you either go out back and chop up some more or drive down to the nearest shop and buy some. In fact, you get plenty of extra so that the next time you want to build a fire you don't have to go back out unless you want to.

Now, imagine this scenario:

> You live wherever it is that you live. Your partner asks you if there's enough money to go on vacation this year, but when you look at the bank account, it's almost empty. What do you do next?

Well, if you're like most people, you panic. You either make up excuses as to why you can't take a vacation or lay down the law about why vacations are overrated and a waste of money anyway. Secretly, you feel like a bit of a failure and resent the heck out of your partner for wanting to go in the first place (even though you'd love to get away as well). Perhaps you vow to yourself to work harder, or find a better-paying job or less demanding partner.

What's the difference between the two scenarios?

In the first, you recognize that wood is just a commodity—something you need from time to time for a specific purpose and that it's easy enough to get more of with a little bit of effort.

In the second, you're acting as if money is in some way magical—something you always need more of and that would make your problems magically disappear if only you could somehow get enough of it.

But what if money were just a commodity, too— something you use from time to time for a specific purpose and that it's easy enough to get more of with a little bit of effort? If money were just a commodity, you wouldn't panic when you were running low—you'd simply go out and get more of it whenever there was something you wanted to buy. You might even get plenty of extra so the next time you wanted to buy something or go somewhere you didn't have to go back out unless you wanted to.

And herein we discover the first part of the secret:

**Financial security doesn't come from
the amount of money you currently have;
it comes from your ability to get
more of it whenever you want.**

The fact is, money and wood (and metal and pork bellies) *are* just commodities. The difference between them is that you buy wood with money and you "buy" money with service.

This gives us the second part of the secret:

**Master the art of serving others
and you will secure your financial future.**

In this sense, money is just a measure of the difference you're making in the world. If you're not making any difference, it will be difficult to make any money.

The Art of Service

1. Who do you currently serve with your work? In other words, who benefits from what you do? What value do you (and your work) create in the lives of others? For example:

"I'm a plumber—my work benefits my clients, the company who sends me out, and my family. I fix leaky pipes and faulty plumbing, but more than that, I help people have hot showers and warm radiators in the winter, and cool air-conditioning and clean tap water in the summer."

"I'm an artist—my work benefits the people who see it, the people who buy it, and the galleries and Websites that display it. The value I create with my art is to bring a sense of beauty and aliveness into the lives of the people who view my art."

---

2. Who else could you serve? What additional differences *could* you make in their lives?

"As a plumber, I could be of service not only to anyone who lives in a house or apartment building but also to companies and even the city I live in. Perhaps there's some way I could be of service to the local utility companies and the hardware stores where people go to try to fix their own plumbing problems.

"I could offer do-it-yourself tips to my customers so that when it's a small problem, they could save money by making the repair themselves. If I got a bit more disciplined about showing up on time and always phoning if there was going to be a delay, I could add 'reliability' to my list of services and 'peace of mind' to the list of benefits I offered. When it's real, people will always pay a premium for that."

"As an artist, I could get my art in front of more people—perhaps offering to loan or even giving paintings to hospitals and corporations where people could really benefit from the inspiration and beauty.

"I could offer classes in art appreciation, maybe even in conjunction with the local museum or library. Not only would people benefit by being able to see more of the subtle nuances that make great art great, those who did buy my art would get even more value from owning it. Also, people who buy art as an investment would be able to become more discerning and make better choices about what they bought (and didn't buy) in the future."

Employee or Creator?

"Life begets life; energy begets energy. It is by spending oneself that one becomes rich."

— attributed to Sarah Bernhardt

Charlie was a professional actress, beautiful and skilled. When she came to me, she had a number of credits in film and television but had yet to make the leap into large-budget movies or regular series work.

In our very first session together, she launched into a diatribe about her agent, her manager, the director of a theater show she had been in, and a producer who was interested in her either professionally or romantically, or both.

Despite wanting to impress her with what a good listener I was, I interrupted after 15 minutes or so with a question: "Where do you think your next job is going to come from?"

This set off another monologue about the problems with being female and over 25 years old in Hollywood, so I tried a different tack: "Where do you think your next great performance is going to come from?"

She finally stopped talking long enough to take some time to think.

"It's going to come from inside me," she said.

"Exactly," I replied. "When you spend all your time and energy trying to get someone to give you an opportunity, you're thinking like an employee. But when you shift your focus to what you can create and what differences you can make in people's lives, you're thinking like a creator. And ironically, the more time you spend thinking like a creator, the more opportunities you'll find knocking at your door."

To make the point more clearly, consider two handymen working on your house. The first does a good professional job, shows up on time, and charges what he said he would. Because he thinks like an employee, when the job is done, he makes a point of letting you know he's available for any future work and then goes home and waits for the phone to ring with the next job. If he's really hungry for work, he may even give you a coupon for a 10 percent discount on the next job.

The second handyman does things differently. He also does a good professional job, shows up on time, and charges what he said he would. But because he thinks like a creator, he's been looking around your house and learning about you. He's noticed that you really love your kids, but that there's not a space in the house you can call your own to relax and unwind in. When the job is done, he comes up to you with a proposal to redo your yard into a combination Zen garden and topiary, filled with animal-shaped shrubbery to delight your children and private spaces ideal for quiet contemplation and relaxation.

"It will cost some money," he tells you, "but if you decide that you'd like it, I'd love to create it for you."

When he goes home, he's not waiting for the phone to ring. He's dreaming up other things he can do with his skills to create more joy and ease in people's lives. Although he's too creatively fulfilled to ever be "hungry" for work, when he wants to make some extra money, he creates specific targeted proposals (like the Zen garden/topiary) and sends them out into the world like invitations. And while not everyone comes to the party, the people who do are delighted by his creations.

$100 in Your Pocket

Here's a question that I taught my friend the supercoach Paul McKenna, a version of which he included in his wonderful book *I Can Make You Rich:*

> *"If you woke up one morning in a place where you knew no one, with $100 in your pocket, how long would it take you to double your money and how would you do it?"*

Once you've answered that question, *how long would it take you to double it again, and how would you do it? And again? And again?*

The more answers you can come up with, the more your financial future is secured. If you think you've run out of ideas, reflect on these words attributed to Thomas Edison: "When you have exhausted all possibilities, remember this—you haven't."

Remember, thinking like a creator has nothing to do with whether or not you currently have a job, or whether or not that job is considered to be "creative." My actress client was incredibly creative, but she still thought like an employee and consequently never saw the possibilities for creation that were all around her.

Similarly, I've worked with a number of people who were able to begin thinking like a creator from within their job. While a few moved on to set up their own businesses, many found ways of creating additional value from within their jobs and began to be rewarded commensurately.

Here are some additional distinctions you may find useful:

When you think like an employee . . .	When you think like a creator . . .
. . . you are reactive.	. . . you are proactive.
. . . you are optimistic or pessimistic.	. . . you are inspired.
. . . you expect to be rewarded for the work you put in.	. . . you expect to be rewarded for the difference you make.
. . . you see others as the source of your income.	. . . you recognize your inspiration, creativity, skill, and effort as the source of your income.

Take some time this week to bring the creative-creator mind-set to life. . . .

The Creative Creator

1. Where in your life are you thinking like an employee, wondering who will finally give you a break, an opportunity, or a job?

Each time you notice yourself getting caught up in an "employee" mentality, make the shift to "creator" mode by asking yourself what you would love to create today.

Here are some questions that will assist you in getting started:

- What could you begin to work on for its own sake?

- What would bring you great joy and meaning if you could bring it into being?

- What would you love to create that people would love to give you money for?

- What is the largest contribution you can imagine making to someone's life? How much would you be willing to be paid for making it?

2. For the next week, purposely create at least one thing each day. It can be as simple as a carefully crafted e-mail or as complex as a painting or sculpture.

3. Create at least three proposals in the next month where you invite people to give you money for something you have or will create. Prepare to be pleasantly surprised by the responses you get.

The Invisible Obstacle to Wealth

> *"The lack of money is the root of all evil."*
>
> — Mark Twain

One of the benefits people are often searching for when they hire me as a coach is a significant increase in their level of wealth—both the amount of income they're able to create and the level of well-being they're able to sustain in creating and maintaining it.

And as with any other creation, creating money is essentially a very simple process:

1. Decide what you want to create.
2. Create it!

If you really want to create money, the only thing that can stop you is a thought. And the thought that more than any other seems to separate the haves from the have-nots, or at least the "have-mores" from the "have-lesses," is so subtle that it's nearly invisible.

I remember when one of my coaches first pointed out that the biggest obstacle to my own wealth was my belief that I needed the money. We reviewed a number of my business dealings over the years, and one by one he pointed out how I'd settled for less than I wanted because I'd thought I had to take whatever was on offer. To my surprise, we also noticed several situations where I'd blown it because my desperate sense of need had been driving me to try to squeeze every last penny out of every deal.

After that, each time I argued that I really did need the money, he would calmly ask me some variation on the question: "What would happen if you didn't get it?" No matter how urgent or important each financial opportunity felt at the time, I would eventually realize that there was always another way forward and that no one opportunity was the be-all and end-all of my financial success.

Now, one of the first questions I ask my own clients is: "How many days forward could you go without earning any money before you would be out on the street?" The answer is generally measured in months or years, not days. (Actually, the most common answer is: "I would never be out on the street, because my family/friends/community would make sure I always had a place to stay until I got back on my feet.")

One client who had been arguing for his "need" for money sheepishly admitted that he could go ten years without working before running out of money. Based on this, we created an experiment. For the next three years, he would proceed in business from the assumption that he didn't need the money. All of his choices over that time period were to be made based on inspiration and true heartfelt desire. In other words, he was going to begin to do what he wanted to do, not what he thought he "should" do or "needed" to do. (We figured that would still give him seven years to go back to doing things out of desperation before he ran out of money!)

Although he struggled with it for several months, before the first year was out he had made more than ten times as much money as he had the year before and was doing work that he really loved and wanted to do.

So how is it that by letting go of neediness he was able to create so much more wealth in his life? And more important, why would someone who clearly didn't need the money continue to act for all the world as if he did?

Let's take a look at each of these questions in turn.

1. Why Do You Make More Money When You Stop Needing It?

As we've already discussed, there are essentially three motivations for anything and everything we do: *desperation, rationalization,* and *inspiration.* In linguistic terms, these usually are expressed in terms of:

- "I'm doing it because I have to." (desperation)
- "I'm doing it because I should." (rationalization)
- "I'm doing it because I want to." (inspiration)

When you act out of a sense of desperation (that is, neediness), you have to settle for whatever is on offer. There's generally a sense of urgency that shifts the balance in any negotiation in the other person's favor. What's more, you feel so uncomfortable in your own skin that you put your worst foot forward, trying too hard to please or shifting to the other side and putting on a front of anger or bravado to cover up your fear.

However, when you act as though you don't need the money (because almost invariably, no matter what your fear has been telling you, you don't), you move forward with a sense of ease and well-being. It's easy to stick to your bottom line because you always have an alternative—getting on with your wonderful life and offering your creativity and skills at difference making and value creation to any of the hundreds, thousands, and sometimes millions of people who would benefit from them.

You enter negotiations without fear, because whether or not you reach agreement, you know at an absolutely fundamental level that your well-being is not dependent on making a deal. And when you're okay with the other person saying "no," you can ask for anything you want.

2. "If I Don't Need the Money, Why Do I Feel So Needy?"

When it comes to money, nearly all of us have learned to protect and motivate ourselves by creating feelings of worry, fear, and even desperation. "If I can just stay scared enough," this internal logic tells us, "I'll be safe and I'll keep moving forward." The problem with this point of view is that fear is one of the least effective states to move forward in—it impairs your reasoning, limits your vision, destroys your health, and gives off a horrible stench that puts people off doing business with you: the sickly smell of desperation.

(Think about it for a moment—who would you rather have working with you on a project? Someone who's inspired to make things happen or someone who's desperate not to mess things up?)

It's at this point in the discussion that someone inevitably says to me, "That's all right for all your wealthy clients, but what if I really *do* need the money?"

Listen, if your children are starving or you're going to lose your apartment or house at the end of the month because you're six months in arrears on the rent or mortgage, do what you need to do to take care of yourself and your family.

But when I push them on it, nearly everyone who seems in dire straits could in reality go on for another three to six months by making a few adjustments in their lifestyle. And three to six months is more than enough time to put your creativity and inspiration to work on creating value, making a difference, and exchanging that value and difference making for money.

Don't Need the Money

1. Review all of your recent business dealings— contract negotiations, proposals put forward, sales calls, or whatever else you do to make money. How much of your motivation was inspiration (doing it because you wanted to), how much rationalization (doing it because you felt you should), and how much was desperation (doing it because you thought you needed to)?

2. Choose one business deal that you don't mind losing. If you don't have any deals pending, make one up—create a proposal that's so outlandish that you would love it if it came through but you really don't need it to, because it's so "out there." Notice the difference in your own energy levels and creativity as you do so.

3. Begin to say no to things you don't want to do by asking for more money. If you really don't want to do them, ask for what seems to you to be a ridiculous amount of money. This will begin to establish a new pattern in your brain of asking for what you want without a sense of neediness.

For example, I had the chance to work with the CEO of an international corporation on her presentation skills. While I wouldn't have minded the work, I wasn't terribly interested in it. Rather than turn it down, I created a $100,000 coaching proposal. (That's about four or five times the going rate.) I was pretty sure she'd reject the proposal, but if she had agreed, I would have happily completed the job.

One word of warning—occasionally, people will say yes to these outrageous proposals, so don't make them if you're truly unwilling to honor your end of the agreement!

Understanding Scarcity

"You don't get what you deserve in life—
you get what you negotiate."

— Chester L. Karrass

Economics is a vast and complex field, but in some ways it can be reduced to one simple principle:

The scarcer the resource, the more people are willing to give up in order to get it; the more common the resource, the less people are willing to give up in order to get it.

That means that on the one hand, a plot of land in the heart of the city will nearly always fetch more than the same size plot in the country; on the other hand, no one would ever bribe the maître d' to get into a McDonald's.

Recent estimates place the wealth of the world at over $44 trillion. Yet the fundamental mistake that nearly everyone makes when it comes to wealth is to think of money as a scarce resource.

Why do we put up with boorish behavior and ignorant decision making from the people above us in our company? Why is the customer "always right"? Because in both cases, they're the ones with the money, and we're seeing ourselves as a common resource in pursuit of a scarce one.

In order to turn that equation around, there are only two things you need to do:

1. See the abundance of money that surrounds you. Years ago I was at a seminar about raising money for film production. When the producer up in front of the room was asked where she intended to get the money for her next movie, she said simply, "From wherever it is now."

Unlike our successful producer, most of us think that our personal sources of income are limited to our jobs, the government, or the generosity of a wealthy relative. We fail to see the opportunities for wealth that surround us every minute of every day.

Here's the simple rule of thumb:

Anywhere there is a positive difference to be made,
there is money to be made.
If you can't (or won't) make any difference,
you're unlikely to make very much money.

How Much Should I Charge?

Some people think the limit on what they can charge has to do with their self-worth, but in fact it simply has to do with what they're willing to ask for. You'll almost never be paid more than you ask for, regardless of how much or how little you happen to believe you're worth.

I've found that most people I work with have a number in their heads that can be accessed with a little prodding.

If you or someone you know isn't sure what to charge for something, play the "higher/lower" game.

Choose any number to start and ask, "Is it [this number]?"

The only three acceptable answers are "Higher," "Lower," or "That's it!"

Keep going until you've determined the perfect price for you.

What's great about this is that you never have to worry about getting it wrong. If it's too much, the marketplace will tell you by not giving you as much business as you want; if it's too little, you'll know because you'll be swamped!

2. **Make yourself a "scarce resource."** Stuart Wilde used to regale us for hours with stories of gas-station attendants who would attract customers from miles around with their five-star-hotel-quality toilets, or purveyors of knickknacks who made hundreds of thousands of dollars from people who wanted to "take home a little piece of the store."

His point was always to begin your quest for wealth by working on yourself—your energy, your skills, and your well-being. "As you become more and more skilled in what you do and happier and happier in yourself," Stuart would say, "people will be drawn to you. They will want to spend time hanging out in your energy. And when they show up—bill 'em!"

The point is this:

As long as you see money as a scarce resource, you will continually inconvenience yourself in order to get it. As soon as you have made *yourself* the scarce resource, the money will inconvenience itself to get you.

In a nutshell:

- Your well-being is not dependent on your bank balance.

- Financial security doesn't come from the amount of money you currently have; it comes from your ability to get more of it whenever you want.

- Master the art of serving others and you'll secure your financial future.

- Don't need the money.

We're almost done! Feel free to reread this chapter or go back through any of the sessions and secrets we've covered up until now.

When you're ready, there's one more session to be had. . . .

SESSION TEN

The Power of Hope

"All dreams appear impossible until someone makes them happen."

— Barry Neil Kaufman

Throwing Starfish

A man was walking along the beach after a storm when he came across an old woman throwing starfish that had washed up onshore back into the sea.

When he asked her what she was doing, she said she'd always wanted to make a difference and had decided that today was a good day to begin.

The man looked from her to the thousands of starfish that lay dying along the coastline and said, "For every starfish you throw back into the ocean, three more wash up onto the shore! How can you possibly be making a difference?"

The woman looked thoughtful for a moment; then she picked up another starfish and threw it back into the sea.

She smiled. "Made a difference to that one."

◆

What One Person Can Do

*"Argue for your limitations, and sure
enough, they're yours."*

— Richard Bach

My friend and mentor Bill Cumming has lived what I consider to be an extraordinary life. After more than 15 years of campaigning in the civil-rights movement and creating a number of programs for individual and team empowerment (including the pilot for the program now known as Upward Bound), his life changed forever when his nine-year-old daughter, Joy, was raped just a few hundred yards from his Ohio home.

At that moment, Bill realized he was fully capable of the kind of violence he had spent so many years campaigning against, and his work turned in a new direction—finding out what the true causes of violence in are our society, and how they can be changed.

During the course of his research, he visited a prison in Somers, Connecticut, and spent time with a group of murderers, rapists, and other violent offenders who had been working with a man named Dr. Nick Groth for over a year. To Bill's surprise, rather than blaming what they'd done on their often horrific upbringings filled with abuse, violence, and criminal neglect, all of these men took full responsibility for their lives.

Toward the end of their time together, one man who had committed three rape/murders and held no possibility of parole took Bill aside and expressed his heartfelt compassion and sorrow for what had happened to Joy.

In that moment, Bill realized that if he was capable of murder and a murderer was capable of that degree of compassion, the capacity for all things must live inside all of us. As he wrote in the course manual for "What One Person Can Do":

> What I learned in this unusual laboratory is that it is possible, given two critical factors, for even the most violent people to develop meaningful, productive, contributory lives, even within the confines of a maximum security prison. The fact that this is so speaks volumes in terms of what we can do. . . .
>
> The critical factor . . . was getting these individuals to know that they were loved (i.e. cared about, valued) and that they were able to make choices. . . . *If it is possible in this environment, with these men, it is possible at every moment in every environment with anyone.*

In private conversation, Bill has told me on numerous occasions that in nearly every instance he has seen where people have turned their lives around, there has been the presence of at least one individual who loved (cared for, valued) them unconditionally and believed in them and in their capacity to choose—to make different choices and fundamentally change the direction, quality, and character of their lives.

At first, I felt that Bill's work was very important but not terribly relevant to my own life. After all, nothing that horrific has ever happened to me or the people I care about most. But I soon came to realize that the same critical factors were present anytime I overcame a crisis in my own life.

"I Believe in You"

Choose a person in your life whom you deeply love and would love to see tap into the power within them.

The next time you spend time with them, decide to be with them as they are, without trying to change, fix, or help them in any way. Know in your heart that no matter what is going on, they have the ability at any moment to spread their wings and go from falling to flying.

My parents believed in my mental strength and capacity at a time when I was so messed up that I thought they were the ones who were nuts for believing in me. Charley Helfert and Dale Moffitt, professors at Southern Methodist University, believed in me enough to not only bring me into their professional-actor training program but to refuse to let me be pushed out even when some of their perhaps more "sensible" colleagues were lobbying for my expulsion. Their belief in me forced me to question my own sense of worthlessness. If *they* thought there was something inside me worth spending time on and salvaging, maybe there really was. In short, they believed in me long enough and consistently enough for me to begin to search inside myself for the strength they seemed to see so effortlessly inside me.

And since I've found that strength and begun to use it to create my own wonderful life, I've felt equally committed to believing in others—to making the choice to treat the people I come into contact with as though they too have the power within them to choose and to change. And because the world is what I think it is, they miraculously and consistently prove me right—again and again and again.

The Tenth Secret

I was teaching a seminar several years back when a woman stood up, dripping with disgust, and pointed an accusatory finger at me. "The problem with you," she said, "is that you give people hope."

She was right, of course, although in my defense it had never occurred to me that this might be perceived as a bad thing.

Where did hope get such a bad name? Criticism of both religion and New Age thinking is filled with accusations of giving people "false hope." But what makes hope false?

The *Oxford American Dictionary* defines *hope* as "a feeling of expectation and desire for a certain thing to happen" and as "grounds for believing that something good may happen." False hope, then, doesn't have to do with my feeling of expectation and desire for my relationships to be successful, my business to make money, and my body to be healthy, but with my grounds for believing that these things are possible.

If I ask you to believe in yourself and your dreams because I have "secret" knowledge of the future that reveals that as long as you do X, Y, and Z, you'll ultimately succeed, that is unfortunately false grounds for hope—I have no such knowledge. However, if I ask you to believe in yourself and your dreams because there are hundreds if not thousands of stories of people who have succeeded in spite of the evidence, that is indeed grounds for legitimate hope, regardless of how things ultimately turn out.

(A quick word on "evidence": in days gone by, the evidence has clearly "proven" that the sun revolves around the earth, which is in fact flat; that bumblebees can't fly; and that humankind will not only never reach the moon, but can't run a mile in less than four minutes or find true and lasting happiness in a world filled with suffering—oh, wait, is that one still a fact?)

Here's my definition of hope and our tenth secret:

Hope is the magic elixir that energizes dreams, fuels possibilities, and lets you live beyond the limits of your historical thinking. It is not a promise that something you want will happen—it is an invitation to enjoy the possibility of what you want while you and life negotiate the eventual outcome.

There is *never* a good reason not to hope.

Why not try the following exercise?

Waking Up Your Dream

There are three kinds of dreams we harbor for our lives:

a. Those we outgrow
b. Those we fulfill
c. Those we give up on

A useful inventory to take from time to time is to reflect on the many dreams you've held for yourself and your life.

1. Make three columns on a piece of paper.

2. Column A is for those dreams for your life that you've outgrown—for example:

- "To be a firefighter."
- "To drive the red and white car from *Starsky and Hutch.*"

- "To take over the *Playboy* empire from Hugh Hefner."

3. Column B is for those dreams you have lived or are living now—for example:

- "I always wanted to live abroad, and I did."
- "I used to dream of having a big soppy dog, and now I live with two of them."
- "I wanted to work alongside my mentors, and now I do."

4. Column C is for those dreams you've given up on, either because you've tried and "failed," because they seem impossible, or because they just seem like too much work—for example:

- "Becoming President of the United States."
- "Recovering from an illness."
- "Becoming a billionaire."
- "Meeting the man or woman of my dreams."

5. Choose to reignite at least one dream from Column C by giving yourself hope. The way you do so is the same way you "make believe" in what you want—simply begin to look for as many "reality"-based reasons as you can find why what you want is indeed possible.

If you want to recover from an illness, for example, you could say:

> "I can give myself hope by focusing on the 'exceptions' to the rule—those people who accepted their diagnosis but rejected the prognosis and lived healthy, productive lives. I can focus on the 'alternative' evidence that shows that every cell in the body is completely replaced every seven years, that what we do with our minds has a significant and measurable effect on what goes on in our bodies, and that seemingly 'mystical' activities like meditation and prayer have consistently brought about healing results that go far beyond 'coincidence.'"

What's Their Dream?

"The greatest good we can do for others is not just to share our riches with them, but to reveal theirs."

— Zig Ziglar

In his book *The Dream Manager,* supercoach Matthew Kelly tells the story of a large cleaning company that solved the problem of high employee turnover by hiring a "dream manager"—in essence an in-house life coach whose job it was to help people articulate their dreams, formulate plans, and follow them through to achievement.

Along the way, he raises an interesting question:

How well do you know the dreams of the people closest to you?

As someone who has worked as a personal and corporate coach for 20 years now, I assumed the answer would be: "Really, really well indeed." But rather than trust my assessment, I decided to actually find out.

First up was my wife. Although I was embarrassed to ask (after all, surely I should know what the woman I love's heart longs for), I was heartened by her clarity about her dreams for us as a family and a few particular personal ones, but I could hear her hesitancy about achieving them. It was then that I realized that one of the most profound ways I could support her was by working with her on making her dreams come true instead of acting as a "devil's advocate" against them. (A complete aside, but does the devil really need an advocate? And if so, is that really whom you want as your employer?)

Next were the kids. Oliver dreams of life in high school and saving up for a Ford Mustang as his first car. Clara wants to sing and act, and Maisy is dead set on becoming a mermaid and then going to medical school.

What makes these dreams so powerful to me is not the impact they would have on the world, but the impact creating them will have on my children. As they learn to discover that they can have what they want (and that what they want may change many times through the course of their lives), they will become what T. E. Lawrence called "dreamers of the day."

As he said in his autobiography:

> All men dream: but not all equally. Those who dream by night in the dusty recesses of their minds wake in the day to find that it was all vanity: but the dreamers of the day are dangerous . . . for they may act their dream with open eyes, to make it possible.

And that's what I want for everyone in my life—my family, my friends, my clients—and yes, even you: that you may act your dreams with open eyes and make them possible.

So I'd like to bring this session and indeed our time together to a close with an invitation—the invitation to become "a believer." A believer is someone who chooses to believe in the capacity inside each one of us to be more than we thought we were capable of—to fly higher and travel harder and arrive triumphantly, creating lives that make us (and often everyone around us) go "Wow!"

There's no movement to join, no manifesto to sign, just a gentle reminder and an open invitation to be the difference-maker in someone else's life and to be open to having that difference made in your own. Tell someone you believe in them. Mean it. Demonstrate it in the way you treat them. Then stand back and watch their life begin to blossom and bloom.

I began this session with a quote from Richard Bach's wonderful book *Illusions:* "Argue for your limitations, and sure enough, they're yours." I'll put it somewhat less poetically, but hopefully with equal strength:

Argue for your possibilities, and sure enough,
you will find much more capacity and ability inside
yourself than you ever dreamed possible.

What's Their Dream?

I think you'll be surprised by how much you enjoy this little experiment. . . .

1. Make a list of the three to five most important people in your life.

2. Take some time this week to ask them about their dreams—what they long for, what they would love, and what would make them go "Wow!"

3. Let them know you're on their side—that you love them, believe in them, and will support and assist them in making their dreams come true.

4. Ask at least three people you don't know well (or even at all!) what their dreams are for their lives.

While not everyone is up for this conversation, the connection you make with the ones who are will make a tremendous difference in your own sense of joy and meaning in your life.

In a nutshell:

- Hope isn't a promise that something you want will happen; it's an invitation to enjoy the possibility of what you want while you and life negotiate the eventual outcome.

- There is *never* a good reason not to hope.

- What if it could work? Yes, but what if it could? What then?

Are You Ready to Become a Supercoach?

"When you were born, you cried and the world rejoiced. Live your life in such a way that when you die, the world cries and you rejoice."

— Indian proverb

The Bodhisattva's Vow

One day, a seeker who had devoted many lifetimes to attaining enlightenment broke through the conditioned thinking of his ordinary mind and saw the world around him as no more than samsara, a projection of his own largely fearful thoughts. His entire being was filled with joy, and he felt as if every cell in his body was dissolving into the bliss of nirvana. It was as though the gates of heaven had opened up to him and he glided effortlessly toward them.

But no sooner had he set one foot in heaven than he heard a sound that filled his heart with compassion. He turned back to see a seemingly infinite number of perfect beings acting for all the world like trapped cattle, struggling to make their way in the world and suffering at the hands of phantoms created by their own minds.

In that moment, he made this vow: "For as long as space endures, and for as long as living beings remain, until then may I too abide to dispel the misery of the world."

To this day, it is said, the Bodhisattva works tirelessly for the liberation of all sentient beings, one foot firmly planted in heaven, the other planted firmly here on Earth.

The Ten Secrets, Revisited

Here are the ten secrets we've been exploring in this book:

1. The world is what you think it is. You are creating your experience of the world moment by moment.

2. Well-being is not the fruit of something you do; it is the essence of who you are. There is nothing you need to change, do, be, or have in order to be happy.

3. There's nowhere for you to get to—you're just *here.*

4. What you decide will never impact your life as much as how you handle the consequences of that decision.

5. Every emotion you experience is a direct response to a thought, not to the world around you.

6. No matter what seems to be going on in your life, you don't *have* to do anything. Everything you do (or don't do) is a choice.

7. You create other people by how you listen to them.

8. You can ask anyone for anything when you make it okay for them to say "no."

9. Financial security doesn't come from the amount of money you currently have; it comes from your ability to get more of it whenever you want. Master the art of serving others and you will secure your financial future.

10. There is *never* a good reason not to hope.

As you begin to gain insight into these secrets for yourself and experience their effects, your life will begin to transform. "Results" will matter less than ever, and you'll find yourself producing them even more consistently. Your fears and stresses will fall away as you recognize that the capacity to create the life you want to live has been inside you right from the very beginning. You may even find that your biggest problem is that you have no more big problems.

As your life gets better and better, it will begin to have a positive impact on the people around you and transform their lives, too. Even if your "job description" isn't part of the helping profession, people will just feel more relaxed in themselves when they're with you. They'll find themselves creating more effortless success in their lives and producing results far beyond their expectations. There is nothing you need to do to make this happen—it's the natural result of resting in your innate well-being and evolving your understanding of how people are creating their experience of whatever it is they're experiencing.

When I was first learning to become a coach, my favorite stories were about the Taoist sages who used to wander from village to village in ancient China. Although these sages held a variety of jobs in a disparate array of professions, they lived in such harmony with themselves and the world around them that whenever they passed through a town, disputes would resolve themselves and problems would be "dis-solved" in the clarity of their presence. Without necessarily working directly to help others, these sages were simply a helping, healing power in the world.

As your understanding of the ten secrets deepens, you'll become like one of these ancient sages—or at least their modern equivalent, a supercoach! While this will bring you untold joys in your life, it will also bring an interesting new responsibility. . . .

The Helper's Dilemma

"Happiness and a meaningful life come from making differences. But this is the most important rule to follow: always make the differences you can make, not the differences you would prefer to make but can't."

— Lyndon Duke

Once upon a time I used to walk out in front of a group to deliver a talk or a workshop with the simple intention of sharing the best of what I knew from my heart. If people liked it and acted on what I suggested, wonderful; if they didn't, well, that was a shame, but "no harm, no foul." But as the years have gone by and more and more people have heard me speak and my books and tips and radio shows have brought me some measure of reputation and authority, I notice that people are now willing to act on my suggestions simply because they're my suggestions. They're more likely to bypass their own inner wisdom in favor of my clever catechisms, using my ideas not as catalysts for their inspiration but as a temporary replacement. "After all," one recent seminar attendee said to me, "you're *you*, and I'm only me!"

This came to a head for me recently when I was speaking at the United Nations to a small group of delegates, spouses, interns, and friends. The talk was an exploration of cultural mythology and how it impacts our pursuit of success and happiness. Afterward, as often happens, people came up to me seeking guidance about situations in their personal lives, ranging from diplomatic issues to weight loss to child rearing. But when one young person approached me wanting to know whether I thought she should "break free of cultural mythology" and give up her virginity before marriage, I found myself face-to-face with every helper's dilemma:

The more successful we become in our desire
to make a positive difference in the world,
the more capable we become of doing damage.

Do we press on with a willingness to "kill one, save many"? Or do we mute ourselves, following the Hippocratic dictum to "first, do no harm"?

I'm a man of my time, so I get my inspiration as often from the movies as I do from ancient philosophical treatises. And I've found my own resolution to this dilemma in the Frank Capra film *It's a Wonderful Life*. In it, Jimmy Stewart's character wishes he had never been born, and his wish is granted. An angel named

Clarence guides him through a vision of a world where his voice has never been heard. And in the darkness of that vision, he becomes reacquainted with his light and the difference he was born to make.

So here's the best of what I know, shared from my heart:

> *You have a wisdom inside you—listen for it and give it voice.*
>
> *You have a light inside you—feel its glow and let it shine.*
>
> *You have the power to speak and act and make things manifest in the world—let your wisdom and light guide you as you do.*

With love and thanks,

Michael

Acknowledgments

On my wedding day, a man I had never seen before came up to me and said, "You owe me, you know. If it wasn't for me, your wife would never have been born." Slightly worried I was stumbling across a dark family secret just moments after joining the family, he went on to tell me his story.

He had been traveling in rural England in the 1950s, and because his watch was running a bit slow, he missed his train. While waiting for the next train to arrive, he bumped into a young woman on the platform. They shared a carriage on that train, and a little over a year later decided to share their lives with one another.

Still not making the connection, I asked him what that had to do with Nina being born. He seemed surprised that I didn't get it. "Well, if I hadn't missed my train, I would never have met my wife, and your wife's parents would never have met each other at our wedding!"

Although there are far more people who contributed to this manuscript than I could possibly acknowledge, including those whose contributions are somewhat obscured by the mists of time, I would like to offer my very public thanks to the following:

Richard Bandler	Martha Beck
Ali Campbell	Steve Chandler
Michele Christensen	Steve Hardison
Kim Hare	Robert Holden
John LaValle	Rich Litvin
Jen Louden	Toni McGuiness
Donald McNaughton	Stuart Wilde

In addition, my deepest gratitude goes to:

- Paul McKenna and Dougray Scott for being my companions (and entertainment) on the flight during which the idea for this book was born.

- Robert Kirby for submitting the proposal before the ink had dried.

- Michelle Pilley, Jo Burgess, Jo Lal, Alex Freemon, Jill Kramer, Christy Salinas, Reid Tracy, and the entire Hay House team for proving time and again that business and pleasure are two sides of the same coin. Special mention to Amy Rose Grigoriou for my favorite cover design ever!

- Lizzie Hutchins for being the best midwife any literary creation could ever hope to have guiding its entry into the world.

- Jessica Kulik, Terri Carey, and Pamela Schott for doing such a wonderful job of taking care of me and my business while I take time to learn and coach and teach and write.

- David Beeler for listening and listening and listening some more as I teased out the stories and themes that fill these pages.

- Kristen Mansheim for both her supercoaching and her super-feedback on some early drafts of the manuscript.

- Syd Banks, Keith Blevens, George and Linda Pransky, Elsie Spittle, Roger Mills, Jack Pransky, and Ami Chen Mills-Naim for teaching me more about life in the last 18 months than I'd learned in the first 40 years.

And most especially to Nina, Oliver, Clara, and Maisy—you are the greatest gifts in my life, and I am truly blessed to get to spend my days with each one of you!

Resources

Throughout the book, I mention a number of super-coaches who have made a tremendous difference in my own life and work. While I can't guarantee that they will impact your life in the way they have impacted mine, I certainly recommend you research them for yourself in order to learn more!

To make this easier, I've created a directory of all these coaches and more on my Website at:

**www.geniuscatalyst.com/
supercoachresources.php**

I've also included recommended books, CDs, and training programs for those of you interested in supercoaching as a profession. You can visit our special training resource site at:

www.supercoachacademy.com

If you'd like to get in touch with me, you may contact me by e-mail at: **michael@geniuscatalyst.com**.

While I can't respond personally to every e-mail, please know that I do read everything that is sent!

ABOUT THE AUTHOR

Michael Neill is an internationally renowned success coach and the bestselling author of *You Can Have What You Want*, *Feel Happy Now!*, the *Effortless Success* audio program and *The Inside-Out Revolution*. He has spent the past 22 years as a coach, adviser, friend, mentor and creative spark plug to celebrities, CEOs, royalty and people who want to get more out of their lives. His books have been translated into 13 languages, and his public talks and seminars have been well received at the United Nations and around the world.

www.supercoach.com

We hope you enjoyed this Hay House book. If you'd like to
receive our online catalogue featuring additional information
on Hay House books and products, or if you'd like to find
out more about the Hay Foundation, please contact:

Hay House UK, Ltd., 292B Kensal Rd., London W10 5BE
Phone: 0-20-8962-1230 • *Fax:* 0-20-8962-1239
www.hayhouse.co.uk • **www.hayfoundation.org**

Published and distributed in the United States by:
Hay House, Inc., P.O. Box 5100, Carlsbad, CA 92018-5100
Phone: **(760) 431-7695** or **(800) 654-5126**
Fax: **(760) 431-6948** or **(800) 650-5115**
www.hayhouse.com®

Published and distributed in Australia by: Hay House Australia Pty.
Ltd., 18/36 Ralph St., Alexandria NSW 2015 • *Phone:* 612-9669-4299
Fax: 612-9669-4144 • www.hayhouse.com.au

Published and distributed in the Republic of South Africa by: Hay
House SA (Pty), Ltd., P.O. Box 990, Witkoppen 2068 • *Phone/Fax:*
27-11-467-8904 • info@hayhouse.co.za • www.hayhouse.co.za

Published in India by: Hay House Publishers India, Muskaan
Complex, Plot No. 3, B-2, Vasant Kunj, New Delhi 110 070 • *Phone:*
91-11-4176-1620 • *Fax:* 91-11-4176-1630 • www.hayhouse.co.in

Distributed in Canada by: Raincoast, 9050 Shaughnessy St.,
Vancouver, B.C. V6P 6E5 • *Phone:* (604) 323-7100
Fax: (604) 323-2600 • www.raincoast.com

Take Your Soul on a Vacation

Visit **www.HealYourLife.com**® to regroup, recharge,
and reconnect with your own magnificence.
Featuring blogs, mind-body-spirit news, and life-changing
wisdom from Louise Hay and friends.

Visit **www.HealYourLife.com** today!